Storybook Cakes

A step-by-step guide to creating enchanting novelty cakes

Lindy Smith

David & Charles

Contents

Introduction

My two children love stories, so it was not difficult to think of different cake themes that would fit the title of this book. I enjoyed putting this collection together, so I hope you'll have as much fun making the cakes as I have done.

I have included a range of cakes to appeal to boys and girls both young and old. The sophisticated Little Mermaid combing her hair has been my daughter Charlotte's favourite right from the pencil-sketch stage. My son Tristan, on the other hand, has been a wonderful source of good ideas and likes all the traditionally boyish cakes in the book, with King Arthur's Castle being his absolute favourite. But the cakes will appeal to all ages too: for the young at heart, the cat lover, anyone who is fascinated by the mystic Middle East or mythology, there is something for everyone in this book.

Levels of skill were also an important consideration when I chose the projects to include. Although several of the cakes require patience and careful modelling, such as the Woodland Fairy, others, such as The Frog Prince, are simpler. Many can be simplified, and for the novice there are cup cakes and variations to explore. Many of the projects are within your capabilities if you read the instructions fully before you begin and follow the project steps carefully.

I expect most of the cakes will be chosen by readers to celebrate children's birthdays, but many are also suitable for adults and teenagers or for other occasions. There are cakes to appeal to everyone, so each cake in the book has a variation; for example, The Runaway Train's variation is a pink Flower Train that would appeal to train-mad little girls. Also, for each cake there are cup cakes decorated to tie in with the theme, and are ideal to give away in party bags.

I have intentionally made some of the cakes highly detailed and others simpler to show you what is possible and to give you ideas, but if you are short of time or prefer to tackle an easier cake, simply make the elements you like and leave out those that are more involved. Some projects include short cuts with suggestions for achieving a great result in a quicker way.

For those who prefer buttercream to sugarpaste, Teddy Tales and Unicorn Myths are covered with buttercream. Both cakes employ different techniques so that the teddy has natural-looking fur whereas the unicorn has a sleek coat. However, if you are not a buttercream fan, you can cover the carved cakes with sugarpaste instead.

How to use this book

Please read the reference section at the front of the book thoroughly; it explains how to begin tackling the cakes as well as some basic techniques. The projects use a variety of implements, and the most frequently used are listed in the Equipment List on pages 8–9. Where I have used specific makes of cutters or decorations, I have added an abbreviation for the name of the supplier in brackets. You will find an abbreviation list at the beginning of Suppliers on page 104.

Recipes for the cakes, including baking times and quantities for various sizes, as well as all the different types of icing used in the book are provided. If you are going to work on a cake that uses a figure, refer to the Face and Figure Modelling section on page 14 before you look at the project in detail. To help you create the cakes, I have provided templates that are actual size (unless noted otherwise) at the back of the book for projects where you will need to cut out a complicated shape. You will also find cutting diagrams to help you cut large cakes into sections, and carving sketches.

For a professional look you will need to use paste colours and dusts, and there are also some good-quality decorations that you may wish to use. These can be obtained from cake-decorating stores or by mail order; suppliers of equipment and ingredients can be found at the back of the book.

I hope that this book will inspire you to be creative. Please don't be afraid to experiment, as it's a great way to learn. Be adventurous – I bet you'll surprise yourself!

Have fun and enjoy!

Lindy

Email: lindy@lindyscakes.co.uk
Website: www.lindyscakes.co.uk

Tackling Cakes

Although you will be keen to get started on one of the fantastic cake projects in this book, take a little time to read this section so that you are familiar with some important and basic points.

PREPARATION

If your cake is to be a creation that you will be proud of, you will need to be fully prepared. Before you start your chosen project read through the instructions carefully so that you understand what is involved and how much time to allow. Make sure you have all the material and items of equipment to hand that you will need to complete the project.

Time planning
Try not to leave everything to the last minute, and plan your decorating time in advance. As the cakes baked from

the recipes in this book last about two weeks, you have about one week to decorate the cake, leaving a week for it to be eaten.

I have split each project into stages to indicate natural breaks in the decorating process; for example, a two-stage project, such as The Frog Prince, could be carved and decorated over a two-day period. Some projects are obviously more involved than others, for example Jolly Pirate and The Storybook, so try to be realistic with what time you have available.

Lining tins
Neatly lined tins (pans) will prevent the cake mixture from sticking and help to ensure a good shape.

1. Measure the circumference of your tin and cut a strip of baking parchment slightly longer than this measurement to allow for an overlap. Make the strip 5cm (2in) deeper than the height of the tin. Fold up 2.5cm (1in) along the bottom of the strip. For a round tin cut this fold with diagonal cuts, for a square/rectangular tin crease the strip at intervals equal to the length of the inside edges of the tin, and then cut the folded section where it is creased into mitres (**A**).

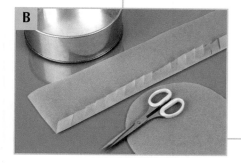

2. Grease the tin and place the strip around the side(s) with the cut edge on the base. Cut a piece of baking parchment to fit the base (**B**), and place in position. For bowls and ball tins, place a small circle of greaseproof paper in the base of the greased bowl/ball.

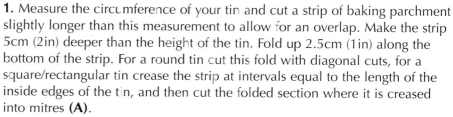
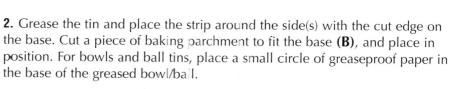

Levelling the cake
Making an accurate cake base is an important part of creating your masterpiece. There are commercial cake levellers available, but I find I get the best results by using a knife and a set square.

Place the set square up against the edge of the cake and, with a knife, mark a line around the top of the cake at the required height, usually between 5cm (2in) and 7.5cm (3in). With a large serrated knife cut around the marked line and across the cake to remove the domed crust (see picture, left).

Freezing and carving cakes

Most of the cake projects require the cakes to be frozen. This allows you not only to bake the cakes in advance but also to carve more intricate shapes without the cake crumbling and falling apart. The corners of the cushion for Cinderella's Slipper, for example, would break off during carving if the cake was unfrozen, and its rounded, realistic shape would be difficult to achieve. How hard your cake freezes will depend on your freezer's settings so it may be necessary to let your cake defrost slightly before attempting to carve.

To cut cakes into different shapes, use a sharp serrated knife and carve off a little at a time until the required shape is achieved (see picture, left). If you remove more than you intended, remedial action can be taken by sticking pieces of cake on again using a little buttercream.

Ready-made decorations

There is an ever-increasing variety of ready-made decorations available from supermarkets and sugarcraft suppliers, and, used wisely, they are a great way of saving time and adding that extra touch. I particularly like the dragées (sugar balls) that I have used on a number of projects in this book, as they add a touch of glamour and opulence to the cakes, such as the decorated heart on Cinderella's Slipper.

Candles

No child's birthday cake would be complete without candles, and there is a huge assortment of styles and colours available as well as novelty candles. Choose carefully to complement the cake so that they will not detract from or spoil your carefully modelled creation. Remember that the candles do not have to be placed on the cake itself, they can be positioned on the board using commercial holders or modelling-paste balls or shapes, such as flowers or stars.

Storage

Protect your cake by placing it in a clean, covered cake box and store somewhere cool and dry, but never in a refrigerator. If the box is slightly larger than the cake and the cake is to be transported, use non-slip matting to prevent the cake moving. Modelling-paste models can be kept forever if placed in a dry, sealed case and stored in the dark. They make a wonderful memento of a special occasion.

The following conditions will affect your decorated cake:

* Sunlight will fade and alter the colours of icing, so always store in a dark place.
* Humidity can have a disastrous effect on decorations, causing the icing to become soft and models to droop. If you live in a humid climate, see the suggested design alterations for the Little Mermaid and Jolly Pirate.
* Heat can melt icing, especially buttercream.

Covering Cakes and Boards

Follow these basic techniques to achieve a neat and professional appearance to the initial cake and board coverings. With care and practice you will soon find that you have a perfectly smooth finish.

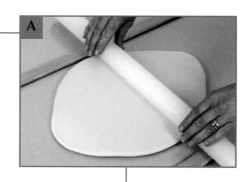

Cakes

Prepare the cake by covering it with a thin layer of buttercream to fill in any holes and help the sugarpaste (rolled fondant) stick (recipes are on page 12).

1. Knead the sugarpaste until warm and pliable. Roll out on a surface lightly dusted with icing (confectioners') sugar, or if you have a large corian work board or worktop use white vegetable fat (shortening) instead. I find white fat works well, and you don't have the problems of icing sugar drying out or marking the sugarpaste. Roll the paste to a depth of 5mm (³⁄₁₆in). It is a good idea to use spacers for this, as they ensure an even thickness **(A)**.

2. Lift the paste carefully over the top of the cake, supporting it with a rolling pin, and position it so that it covers the cake **(B)**. Smooth the surface of the cake to remove any lumps and bumps using a smoother (see page 8) for the flat areas and a combination of smoother and the palm of your hand for the curved ones **(C)**. Always make sure your hands are clean and dry with no traces of icing sugar before smoothing. Trim away the excess paste with a palette knife **(D)**; it often helps to make a cutting line with a smoother, by pressing the smoother down around the edge of the cake into the excess paste before trimming.

If you find you have unwanted air bubbles under the icing, insert a clean glass-headed dressmakers' pin at an angle and press out the air.

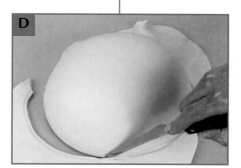

Boards

Roll out the sugarpaste to a depth of 4mm (⅛in), ideally using spacers. Moisten the board with water or sugar glue. Lift up the paste and drape over the board. Circle a smoother over the paste to achieve a smooth, flat finish to the board. Cut the paste flush with the sides of the board, taking care to keep the edge vertical. The covered board should then be left overnight to dry thoroughly.

Tip

You can make your own spacers from strip wood available from DIY stores.

Equipment List

*T*he following is a list of items of equipment that have been frequently used in the book. There are many other sugarcraft items available that you can experiment with. Details can be obtained from the suppliers listed at the back of the book.

Cocktail stick (toothpick) used to add tiny patterns and details and to transfer small amounts of paste colour (**1**).

Craft knife for intricate cutting tasks (**2**).

Cutters
- Circle, plastic and large metal for cutting modelling paste (**3**).
- Heart, for making hearts, such as the decoration for Cinderella's Slipper, and used to create smiles on fun heads (**4**).
- Shield (FMM), used on castle board and cupcakes (**5**).
- Zigzag (FMM), for a zigzag pattern, such as on King Arthur's Castle, The Runaway Train and Noah's Ark (**6**).
- Heart plunger, for adding tiny heart detail (**7**).
- Animal Tappit (FMM), used to cut animals for the Noah's Ark cup cakes (**8**).
- Special Occasion Tappits (FMM), used to make Spooky Ghost and The Storybook cup cakes (**9**).
- Star (PC), used to cut or emboss paste (**10**).
- Pumpkin (PC) (not shown), for adding interesting detail to Hallowe'en cup cakes, and bat (**11**).
- Bird (PC), used to cut small birds for The Storybook cake (**12**).

Dowel for giving extra support to cakes, such as Flying Witch (**13**).

Edible pen for writing messages on cakes (not shown).

Embossers
- Stone wall (FMM), to create a realistic stone wall easily (**14**).
- Green pan scourer, to add texture to paste (**15**). Different scourers have different textures, so experiment with metal and synthetic ones.
- Mini-embossers (HP), for adding embossed detail, such as Noah's Ark and Woodland Fairy (**16**).

Foam use small pieces for supporting modelling paste during drying. Use undulated foam to dry paste in interesting shapes, such as the flags in King Arthur's Castle (**17**).

Measuring spoons for accurate measuring of ingredients (**18**).

Moulds
- Sea shore (DP), for creating realistic shells, as for the rock in Little Mermaid (**19**).
- Teddy (DP), for moulding small teddies for the teddy cup cakes (**20**).
- Head mould (HP), for creating realistic faces, such as Woodland Fairy and Little Mermaid (**21**).

Paintbrushes, including stippling, a range of sizes is useful for painting and dusting cakes (**22**).

Paint pallet for mixing paste food colours together prior to any painting stages (**23**).

Palette knife used for cutting sugarpaste (**24**).

Piping tubes (tips) for piping buttercream and royal icing and for embossing soft paste (**25**).

Reusable piping bag to hold the buttercream or royal icing whilst piping. The coupler is connected to the piping bag and allows the piping tube to be changed easily (**26**).

Ribbon cutter, multisized, time-saving tool for cutting even strips of paste (**27**).

Rolling pins
- Plain large, for rolling out sugarpaste to cover a cake (**28**).
- Small, for rolling out modelling paste and pastillage (**29**).
- Textured (HP), for adding fabric effects to paste (**30**).

Scissors for cutting templates and trimming paste to shape (**31**).

Smoother helps to create a smooth and even finish to sugarpaste (**32**).

Sugar shaper creates pieces of uniformly shaped sugarpaste (**33**).

Sugar shaper discs a selection of shapes to create different effects (**34**).

Spacers narrow and 5mm (³⁄₁₆in), for rolling out paste (**35**).

Tins (pans)
- Round, for baking round cakes **(36)**.
- Multisized, for baking any square or rectangular cake from 2.5cm (1in) to 30cm (12in) **(37)**.
- Ball tin, an excellent way to achieve a perfect sphere **(38)**.
- Food can, a good alternative to cake tins, used for the turrets on King Arthur's Castle **(39)**.

Tools
- Ball tool, makes even indentations, such as eyes, prior to adding detail **(40)**.
- Dresden tool, to create markings on paste, such as the rocks for Little Mermaid **(41)**.
- Cutting wheel, used instead of a knife to avoid dragging the paste **(42)**.
- 'U' tool, used to open up the mouths of realistic faces **(43)**.

Work board, non-stick, used for rolling out modelling paste and pastillage **(44)**.

Piping tubes
The following piping tubes have been used in the book. As tube numbers may vary with different suppliers, always check the tube diameter:

Tube no.	Diameter
0	0.75mm (½in)
1	1mm (⅓₂in)
2	1.5mm (¹⁄₁₆in)
3	2mm (³⁄₃₂in)
4	3mm (⅛in)
16	5mm (³⁄₁₆in)
17	6mm (¼in)
18	7mm (⁵⁄₁₆in)

aking Cakes

Madeira cake

A firm, moist cake that is ideal for carved novelty cakes. It will keep for up to two weeks; I allow one week to decorate and one for it to be eaten. See facing page for the recipe.

1. Pre-heat the oven to 160°C/325°F/Gas 3. Grease and line the cake tin (pan) or bowl with baking parchment (page 5).

2. Cream the butter and sugar in a large mixing bowl until light, fluffy and pale. Sift the flours together in a separate bowl.

3. Beat the eggs into the creamed mixture, one at a time, following each with a spoonful of flour, to prevent the mixture curdling.

4. Sift the remaining flour into the creamed mixture and fold in carefully with a large metal spoon.

5. Transfer to the lined bakeware and bake. When the cake is ready it will be well risen, firm to the touch and a skewer inserted into the centre will come out clean.

6. Allow the cake to cool then, leaving the lining paper on, wrap the cake in foil or place in an airtight container for at least 12 hours before cutting, to allow the cake to settle.

Flavourings

Traditionally, Madeira cake was flavoured with lemon, but it can also be made with other flavourings (flavourings are given for a six-egg quantity Madeira cake; increase or decrease the amounts for other quantities):

Lemon: grated rind of 2 lemons
Cherry: 350g (12oz) glacé (candied) cherries, halved
Fruit: 350g (12oz) sultanas, currants, raisins or dates
Coconut: 110g (3¾oz) desiccated (dry unsweetened shredded) coconut
Nut: replace 250g (9oz) flour with ground almonds, hazelnuts, walnuts or pecan nuts

Chocolate cake

This is a rich, moist yet firm chocolate cake. The secret to success is to use good-quality chocolate with a reasonably high cocoa solids content; I use luxury plain Belgian chocolate with a cocoa solid content of around 50 per cent, which works well. See facing page for the recipe.

1. Preheat oven to 180°C/350°F/Gas 4. Grease and line the cake tin (pan) with baking parchment. See page 5.

2. Melt the chocolate either in a double boiler or in a microwave. Cream the butter and sugar in a large mixing bowl until light, fluffy and pale.

3. Gradually add the egg yolks, then the melted chocolate. In a separate bowl, whisk the egg whites to soft peaks. Gradually whisk the icing sugar into the egg whites.

4. Sift the flour into another bowl and, using a large metal spoon, fold the flour alternatively with the egg whites into the chocolate mixture.

5. Transfer the mixture into the lined bakeware and bake. Baking times will depend on your oven, the cake tin used and the depth of the cake. I usually check the cake after an hour depending on its size. When the cake is baked it will be well risen, firm to the touch and a skewer inserted into the centre will come out clean.

6. Allow the cake to cool then, leaving the lining paper on, wrap the cake in foil or place in an airtight container for at least 12 hours before cutting to allow the cake to settle.

Tip

Break each egg into a cup to prevent small pieces of eggshell falling into the batter.

Cup cakes

Ready made cup cakes are useful, but home-made taste better. See facing page for the recipe.

Prepare the Madeira cake mixture (see 1–4 above). Line bun trays with fluted paper baking cases and fill each half-full. Bake for approximately 20 minutes. Let the cakes stand in the trays for 5 minutes before transferring to a rack to cool completely.

CAKES (Madeira)	BAKEWARE	EGGS (LARGE) (US EXTRA LARGE)	UNSALTED (SWEET) BUTTER	CASTER (SUPERFINE) SUGAR	SELF-RAISNG (SELF-RISING) FLOUR	PLAIN (ALL-PURPOSE) FLOUR	BAKING TIMES at 160°C/325°F/ Gas 3
Cup Cakes	36 cup cake cases	4	225g (8oz)	225g (8oz)	225g (8oz)	125g (4½oz)	20 minutes
Woodland Fairy page 82	1 litre (1¾ pint) pudding basin	4	225g (8oz)	225g (8oz)	225g (8oz)	125g (4½oz)	1¼–1½ hours
Little Mermaid page 46	3 litre (5¼ pint) ovenproof bowl	6	350g (12oz)	350g (12oz)	350g (12oz)	175g (6oz)	1¼–1½ hours
The Runaway Train page 92	23 x 18cm (9 x 7in) rectangular tin (pan) (multisized cake pan)	6	350g (12oz)	350g (12oz)	350g (12oz)	175g (6oz)	1¼–1½ hours
The Frog Prince page 26	23cm (9in) square tin	8	450g (1lb)	450g (1lb)	450g (1lb)	225g (8oz)	1½ hours
Noah's Ark page 40	24 x 16.5cm (9½ x 6½in) ovenproof oval dish plus 15cm (6in) square tin	9	500g (1lb 2oz)	500g (1lb 2oz)	500g (1lb 2oz)	250g (9oz)	oval: 1½–1¾ hours; square: 1 hour
Dick Whittington's Cat page 88	23 x 18cm (9 x 7in) and 13 x 10cm (5 x 4in) rectangular tins (multisized cake pan)	9	500g (1lb 2oz)	500g (1lb 2oz)	500g (1lb 2oz)	250g (9oz)	1–1½ hours
The Story Book page 20	23 x 30cm (9 x 12in) rectangular tin (multi-sized cake pan)	9	500g (1lb 2oz)	500g (1lb 2oz)	500g (1lb 2oz)	250g (9oz)	1½ hours
Arabian Nights page 52	15cm (6in) round tin and 20 x 15cm (8 x 6in) rectangular tin (multisized cake pan)	9	500g (1lb 2oz)	500g (1lb 2oz)	500g (1lb 2oz)	250g (9oz)	1¼–1½ hours
Unicorn Myths page 78	25.5 x 23cm (10 x 9in) rectangular tin (multisized can pan)	9	500g (1lb 2oz)	500g (1lb 2oz)	500g (1lb 2oz)	250g (9oz)	1½–1¾ hours
King Arthur's Castle page 36	25.5 x 12.5cm (10 x 4⅞in) rectangular tin and 8 x 7.5cm (3in) diameter food cans	10	550g (1¼lb)	550g (1¼lb)	550g (1¼lb)	275g (10oz)	1–1¼ hours
Teddy Tales page 68	20cm (8in) round tin, 15cm (6in) round tin plus 10cm (4in) diameter ball tin	10	550g (1¼lb)	550g (1¼lb)	550g (1¼lb)	275g (10oz)	1–1½ hours

CAKES (Chocolate)	BAKEWARE	EGGS (LARGE) (US EXTRA LARGE)	PLAIN (SEMISWEET) CHOCOLATE	UNSALTED (SWEET) BUTTER	CASTER (SUPERFINE) SUGAR	ICING (CONFECTIONERS') SUGAR	SELF-RAISING (SELF-RISING) FLOUR	BAKING TIMES at 180°C/350°F/ Gas 4
Flying Witch page 72	Medium tiffin tin 16cm wide x 13cm high (6¼ wide x 5in high)	4	115g (4oz)	75g (3oz)	175g (6oz)	25g (1oz)	115g (4oz)	1 hour
Spooky Ghost page 58	Medium tiffin tin 16cm wide x 13cm high (6¼in wide x 5in high)	4	115g (4oz)	75g (3oz)	175g (6oz)	25g (1oz)	115g (4oz)	1 hour
Cinderella's Slipper page 62	20cm (8in) square tin	9	250g (9oz)	175g (6oz)	350g (12oz)	75g (3oz)	250g (9oz)	1¼ hours
Jolly Pirate page 30	18 x 30cm (7 x 12in) rectangular tin (multisized cake pan) and a 7.5cm (3in) round food can	10	275g (10oz)	175g (6oz)	400g (14oz)	100g (3½oz)	275g (10oz)	1¼–1½ hours

Sugar Recipes

Most of the sugar recipes used in the book for covering, modelling and decoration can easily be made at home. Use paste colours to colour them according to the individual project.

Sugarpaste

Ready-made sugarpaste (rolled fondant) can be obtained from supermarkets and cake-decorating suppliers, and is available in white and the whole colour spectrum. It is also easy and inexpensive to make your own.

Ingredients Makes 1kg (2¼lb)
60ml (4 tbsp) cold water
20ml (4 tsp/1 sachet) powdered gelatine
125ml (4fl oz) liquid glucose
15ml (1 tbsp) glycerine
1kg (2¼lb) icing (confectioners') sugar, sieved,
  plus extra for dusting

1. Place the water in a small bowl, sprinkle over the gelatine and soak until spongy. Stand the bowl over a pan of hot but not boiling water and stir until the gelatine is dissolved. Add the glucose and glycerine, stirring until well blended and runny.

2. Put the icing sugar in a large bowl, make a well in the centre and slowly pour in the liquid ingredients, stirring constantly. Mix well. Turn out on to a surface dusted with icing sugar and knead until smooth, sprinkling with extra icing sugar if the paste becomes too sticky.

3. The paste can be used immediately or tightly wrapped and stored in a plastic bag until required.

Royal icing

Use royal icing to pipe fine detail.

Ingredients Makes 1 quantity
1 egg white
250g (9oz) icing (confectioners') sugar, sifted

Put the egg white in a bowl and gradually beat in the icing sugar until the icing is glossy and forms soft peaks.

Modelling paste

This versatile paste keeps its shape well, dries harder than sugarpaste and is used throughout the book for adding detail to covered cakes. Although there are commercial pastes available, it is easy and a lot cheaper to make your own.

Ingredients Makes 225g (8oz)
5ml (1 tsp) gum tragacanth
225g (8oz) sugarpaste (rolled fondant)

Add the gum tragacanth to the sugarpaste and knead in (see picture, below). Wrap in a plastic bag and allow the gum to work before use. You will begin to feel a difference in the paste after an hour or so, but it is best left overnight. The modelling paste should be firm but pliable with a slight elastic texture. Kneading the modelling paste makes it warm and easy to work with.

Modelling-paste tips

- Gum tragacanth is a natural gum available from cake-decorating suppliers.
- Placing your modelling paste in a microwave for a few seconds is an excellent way of warming it for use.
- If you have previously added a large amount of colour to your paste and it is consequently too soft, an extra pinch or two of gum tragacanth will be necessary.
- If your paste is crumbly or too hard to work, add a touch of white vegetable fat (shortening) and a little boiled water, and knead until softened.

Sugar sticks

These are used to give edible support to models. If you are pushed for time, pieces of raw dried spaghetti are a good alternative.

Place some soft pastillage in a sugar shaper fitted with the medium round disc and squeeze out straight lengths of paste (see picture, below). Allow to dry thoroughly.

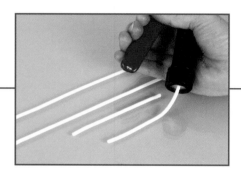

Buttercream

Used to sandwich cakes together, to coat them before covering with sugarpaste or on its own as a cake covering.

Ingredients Makes 1 quantity
110g (3¾oz) unsalted (sweet) butter
350g (12oz) icing (confectioners') sugar
15–30ml (1–2 tbsp) milk or water
a few drops of vanilla extract or alternative flavouring

1. Place the butter in a bowl and beat until light and fluffy.

2. Sift the icing sugar into the bowl and continue to beat until the mixture changes colour. Add just enough milk or water to give a firm but spreadable consistency.

3. Flavour by adding the vanilla or alternative flavouring, then store in an airtight container until required.

White buttercream

An alternative for those on a dairy-free diet, white buttercream is used for coating the unicorn in Unicorn Myths. Simply follow the buttercream recipe but replace the butter with solid white vegetable fat (shortening).

Chocolate buttercream

To make chocolate buttercream, follow the buttercream recipe above and mix 30ml (2 tbsp) of unsweetened cocoa powder with the milk or water before adding it to the butter and sugar mixture.

Pastillage

This is an extremely useful paste because, unlike modelling paste, it sets extremely hard and is not affected by moisture the way other pastes are. However, the paste crusts quickly and is brittle once dry. You can buy it in a powdered form, to which you add water, but it is easy to make yourself.

Ingredients Makes 350g (12oz)
1 egg white
300g (11oz) cups icing (confectioners') sugar, sifted
10ml (2 tsp) gum tragacanth

1. Put the egg white into a large mixing bowl. Gradually add enough icing sugar until the mixture combines together into a ball. Mix in the gum tragacanth, and then turn the paste out on to a work surface and knead the pastillage well.

2. If you require some softer pastillage to make items using a sugar shaper, place a portion to one side. Incorporate the remaining icing sugar into the remainder of pastillage to give a stiff paste.

3. Store pastillage in a polythene bag placed in an airtight container in a refrigerator for up to one month.

Sugar glue

Although commercially available, sugar glue is quick and easy to make at home.

Break up pieces of white modelling paste into an eggcup or small bowl and cover with boiling water. Stir until dissolved. This produces a thick, strong glue, which can be easily thinned by adding some more cooled boiled water. If strong glue is required, use pastillage rather than modelling paste as the base (useful for delicate work, but not needed for any projects in this book).

Confectioners' glaze

Used to add a realistic gloss to the eyes of figures and where a glossy-looking sheen is needed, such as The Frog Prince, confectioners' glaze is available from cake-decorating suppliers.

Face and Figure Modelling

*T*he Storybook, Little Mermaid and Woodland Fairy cakes all use figures, and these can be *adapted to personalize the cakes by simply matching the eye colour to the child's and adding hair in the same style and colour. Children love to see themselves portrayed on cakes, so I have given you the option of making either fun, cheeky faces or a more lifelike option.*

Making and adjusting the lifelike head

Knead some flesh-coloured modelling paste, adding a trace of white vegetable fat (shortening). Make a suitable sized ball, roll it into a cone and press the point of the cone firmly into the head mould you are using; the cakes in this book all use the large mould (HP, adult head mould) **(A)**. Shape the back of the head, but don't worry about any marks in the paste, as the hair will cover these. Remove the head from the mould **(B)**. You can use the head as it comes straight out of the mould, but I like to adjust the features of my figures to add more character, as follows:

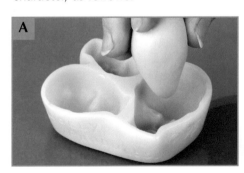

1. Using a Dresden tool, extend the chin by stroking the paste from under the chin forwards **(C)**. Then square the chin slightly by pinching it into shape with your fingers.

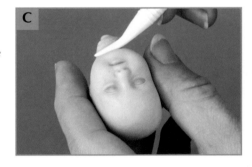

2. Next, define the cheeks with a Dresden tool, by pressing the tool in a diagonal from the nostril to the side of the mouth **(D)**. Then gently smooth the paste of the cheeks into the correct position for your chosen expression, I find it often helps to have a willing volunteer at this stage.

3. Open the mouth by holding a 'U' tool at an angle to the face and pulling the bottom lip down fractionally **(E)**. Then, using a Dresden tool, restore the corners of the mouth to their correct position to make a smile **(F)**.

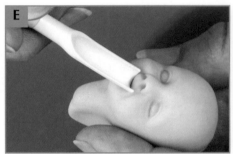

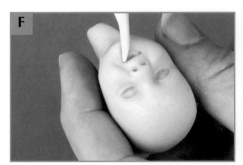

Tip

For ease of modelling, I hold the heads upside down while I adjust the features.

4. Insert a pin into a nostril and gently circle to enlarge, and then pull down to the outside. Repeat for the other nostril **(G)**.

Once you are happy with the shape of the head, cut off the neck and insert a sugar stick. Leave to dry.

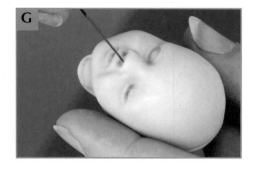

Adding ears

1. Take two small balls of paste and stick them to the sides of the head; the top of the ears should be in line with the eyebrows, and the earlobes in line with the tip of the nose.

2. To shape the ear, press the broader end of a Dresden tool on to the centre of the ball and drag it carefully sideways so the edge of the ball is blended into the face and the remaining paste forms a 'C' shape **(H)**. Press the sharp end of a Dresden tool into the ear to form the ear canal.

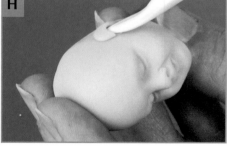

Painting the face

1. To paint the face, dilute suitable paste colours in clear spirit and use a fine paintbrush (I use a no. 00) to paint the detail.

2. For the eyes, start by painting the whites; the mould indicates where these should be. Then paint the background colour of the iris, for example, a pale brown or pale blue, and then add details to the iris, such as a dark rim around the outside. Paint the pupil in the centre of the eye; remember that large pupils look more endearing. Allow the paste colours to dry.

3. With a fine paintbrush, paint eyelashes, eyebrows and lips in suitable colours.

Paint over each eye with confectioners' glaze to make the eyes reflective, and then add small, white light spots to each, making sure they are in the same position on each eye.

Tip

An airing cupboard is an excellent place to dry out models.

4. Finally, brush the cheeks with skin tone/pink dust colours **(I)**.

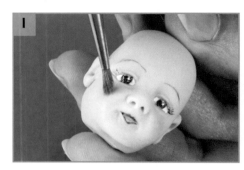

Alternative fun head

Make this simpler head when time is short or a fun head is more appropriate.

1. Knead some flesh-coloured modelling paste to warm it, then roll into a 2.5cm (1in) ball. Holding a cutter at 45 degrees, indent a mouth (**J**).

2. Make the corners of the mouth by using a small circle cutter, piping tube or cocktail stick (toothpick). Try using different cutters to create different expressions (**K**).

3. Indent eyes with a cocktail stick and add a small ball of paste for a nose. Leave to dry thoroughly before adding ears, as described on page 15, and small balls of black paste for the eyes (**L**).

Torso

1. Place the body template in a plastic sleeve. Take a large ball of flesh-coloured modelling paste, and roll it into a sausage the width of the shoulders on the template. Roll the top of the sausage between two fingers to form the neck (**M**).

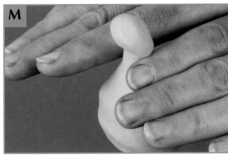

2. Place the paste over the template and stroke the paste down the body until it fits within the lines. Take a palette knife and cut away the excess paste along the marked lines (**N**).

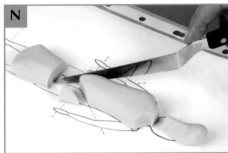

3. Remove the body from the template and round the straight edges of the back back by smoothing them with your fingers. Insert a sugar stick or a length of dried spaghetti through the body to help support the head, and dry supported in an upright position.

Legs

1. Roll a tapered sausage to fit the template roughly (**O**). Shape the ankle by rolling and thinning the paste between your fingers. Create the foot by squeezing the paste to form the toes and pinching it to form the heel. Then take a pair of scissors and make four small cuts to form five toes. Mark nails by indenting each toe with a Dresden tool.

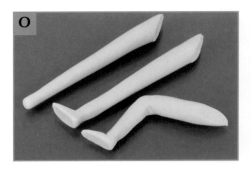

2. For the knee, gently roll the sausage diagonally above and below the joint, then bend to the required position. Replace the leg on the template and cut the top of the leg to fit. Repeat for the second leg.

Arms

1. Roll a tapered sausage of flesh-coloured modelling paste to fit the template. Roll and thin the paste to shape the wrist (**P**). Flatten the hand and, with a pair of small scissors, cut out a small triangle to form the thumb. Cut the fingers and gently roll each to shape, and then mark the fingernails with the tip of a Dresden tool. Cup the hand slightly using a ball tool.

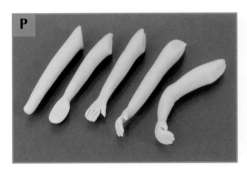

2. Place the arm back on the template and then roll and thin the paste to form the elbow. Place on the template again and cut the arms to the required length, ensuring that the hand is in the correct position before making the angular cut.

Using Colour

The cakes in this book have immediate visual impact owing to the range of colours I have used. Being able to choose a variety of colours, from muted shades to bold and vivid tones, will give you tremendous scope to bring your cakes alive. Flexibility in the range of colours you can use will give you inspiration with your creations, so it helps to know the basics about colour theory and how to mix your own colours when painting or colouring paste.

The colour spectrum consists of three primary colours – red, blue and yellow – from which all colours are made. Therefore, in theory, any colour can be achieved through a combination of these primary colours with the addition of black and white.

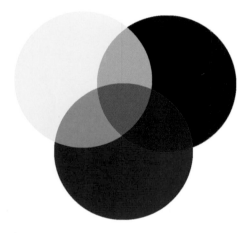

Above: *basic colour mixing.*

Colouring sugarpaste

Brightly coloured sugarpaste (rolled fondant) in all kinds of colours is now available commercially. However, if you can't find the colour you're searching for, or if only a small amount of a colour is required, it is often best to colour your own paste.

Tip

Try to colour your paste in natural light, as artificial light greatly alters certain colours.

Depending on the amount of paste you wish to colour and depth of colour required, place a little paste colour, not liquid colour, on the end of a cocktail stick (toothpick) or a larger amount on the end of a palette knife. Add the colour to the paste and knead in thoroughly, adding more until the desired result is achieved (see picture, top right). Be careful with pale colours, as only a little colour is needed. Deep colours, on the other hand, require plenty

and will become quite sticky. To overcome this, add a pinch of gum tragacanth and leave for an hour or two; the gum will make the paste firmer and easier to handle. Note: the coloured paste will appear slightly darker when dry.

Painting

I often paint over my cakes, as many fabulous effects can be achieved by painting dried sugarpaste. Painting also helps to brighten the overall appearance of a cake, as even vividly coloured paste will dry with a dull finish. Food colours behave in much the same way as ordinary water-based paints, so you can mix and blend them to produce many different tones and hues.

To paint sugarpaste, dilute some paste colour in clear spirit, such as gin or vodka, and, using a paintbrush, a damp natural sponge or stippling brush, apply to the dry sugarpaste. For deep colours, add a little clear spirit to some paste colour. For light colours, or if you want to apply a colour wash, add a little colour to some clear spirit. For details of flood-painting technique see Unicorn Myths, Colouring the Board, on page 78.

Paste colours and dusts

For sugarcraft, paste colours, and not liquid colours, are used to add colour to sugarpaste, modelling paste and pastillage. Dust colours can be mixed with clear spirit or confectioners' glaze and painted on to dry sugarpaste or dusted on with a dry paintbrush to add a light shade or a lustre finish. Dusts are available in a variety of types and colours and are usually used for adding finishing touches, such as skin tone brushed on the cheeks of faces, the copper lustre dust applied to the wings of the Woodland Fairy and the golden Frog Prince's crown.

The Cakes

The Storybook

*A*ll children love stories, and the idea of a storybook cake opens up new worlds of exciting adventures. The magical atmosphere created by this cake is achieved by including a variety of storybook themes, such as the unicorn, moonlit tower, tangled rose thorns and teddies by a cottage, most of which have been made using cutters. Two children look on as they enter the world of make-believe. The size of the cake can easily be enlarged, and the decoration can be personalized.

Materials

Madeira cake made with 9 eggs and baked in a
23 x 30cm (9 x 12in) rectangular cake tin (pan)
(a multisized cake pan is ideal) or bake your cake
in a pre-formed tin (W) (see page 10)
sugarpaste (rolled fondant): 1kg (2¼lb) navy blue,
1.35kg (3lb) cream, 125g (4½oz) green
modelling paste: 50g (2oz) flesh, 15g (½oz) navy
blue, 75g (3oz) grey, 25g (1oz) black, 100g
(3½oz) pale brown, 25g (1oz) white, 75g (3oz)
green, 100g (3½oz) red, 25g (1oz) purple
edible dusts: peach, blue lustre, gold lustre, snowflake
1 quantity buttercream
paste colours: cream, selection of blues, selection
of greens, selection of browns, black
clear spirit, such as gin or vodka
white vegetable fat (shortening)
small amount of royal icing
2 sugar sticks
confectioners' glaze

Equipment

35.5 x 25.5cm (14 x 10in) rectangular cake board
cutters: for the figures' mouths, fish cutter (PC
Water Lily set), unicorn (PC), penguin (PC), bat,
cat and moon (PC Halloween set), teddies and
birds (PC Cradle set), sun (FMM Special Occasions,
Tappits), roses (PC), star (PC Shepherds set)
waxed paper
cutting wheel
stippling brush and paintbrushes
narrow spacers made from 1.5mm (⅟₁₆in) card
set square
black edible pen
smoother
pan scourer
mini-brick embosser (PC)
sugar shaper with small round and mesh discs
piping bag with no. 0 piping tube (tip)

PREPARATION

Preparing a rectangular cake for freezing

If you have not baked your cake in a pre-formed tin **(A)**, remove the crust from the rectangular cake and level to a height of 5cm (2in). Freeze overnight.

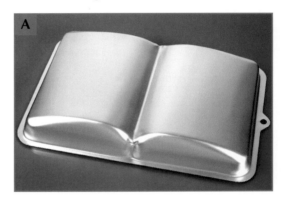

Covering the board

Place the cake board on top of an object, such as a smaller board or plate, to lift it off your work surface. Roll out the navy-blue sugarpaste and use to cover the board, bringing the paste over the edges. Trim the paste flush with the base of the board. Place to one side to dry.

Heads

Make two heads from 3cm (1⅛in) balls of flesh modelling paste following the easy head instructions on page 16 **(B)**. Dust the cheeks with peach lustre dust.

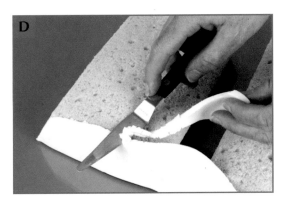

STAGE 1

Carving the frozen cake

1. For a rectangular cake, mark a line 2.5cm (1in) in from both 23cm (9in) sides, then create the sloping pages by cutting from this line to the base (see sketch). Mark the central spine of the book and cut vertically in half. Next carve the top of the cake into a slight curve using the sketch as a guide. Finally, remove a 2cm (¾in) wedge from the spine area **(C)**.

2. If you are using a pre-formed tin, you may wish to cut away the spine area, as above.

Covering the cake

1. Place the cakes on waxed paper. Roll out some cream sugarpaste into a 13cm (5in) wide strip, and cut lengthways into two. Spread buttercream over the two spine areas and cover with the strips, placing the cut edge at the base of the cake. Cut the paste flush with the edges of the cake. Cover the top and bottom of the book pages in the same way **(D)**. Then cover the remaining cake, cutting the paste flush with the sides already covered and blending away the joins with the heat of a finger.

Tip

If the edges of the spine are not completely straight, once the sugarpaste has dried take a straightedge and craft knife and cut vertically through the paste to give edges that will abut each other.

2. To mark the pages, take a straightedge and press it repeatedly into the paste along the long sides of the book. For the ends of the pages, indent a few straight lines for the pages nearest the cover then, with a cutting wheel, start to mark more lines that curve upwards towards the open page.

Tip

To help you mark the lines for pages, open a large book at the centre and copy the way the pages rest.

Cup Cakes

Cover each cup cake with a disc of blue sugarpaste. Thinly roll out cream, yellow and red modelling paste and cut out open-book and sun shapes using cutters (FMM Special Occasions, Tappits). Paint each book and sun with dilute paste colours and position one on each cake.

STAGE 2

Painting the cake

1. Place the cake on the prepared cake board so that the spine areas abut. Mark lines on the board to represent the folds in the book cover at the spine.

2. Dilute some cream paste colour in clear spirit and use to place a weak colourwash over the edges of the pages to give the book an old and well-used look. Next, separately dilute the blue and green paste colours, then, using a stippling brush, stipple over the pages of the book. Stipple blue over the sky area and green for the grass **(E)**, but leave a panel blank on the left-hand page for the text. Use different strengths of colour for different areas, and if you wish to soften the effect, stipple over the painted area with a dry brush. Leave to dry.

STAGE 3

Lettering

1. Roll out the navy-blue modelling paste between narrow spacers. Emboss the paste twice with the fish cutter then carefully cut around each fish with a craft knife.

2. Arrange the fish on your work board into an 'O' shape, and then, using a soft brush, dust over the fish with blue and gold lustre dusts **(F)**. Place the fish on the cake in the top left-hand corner of the area you have left blank for the text. (See page 25 for more lettering ideas.)

3. Take a set square and use this with a craft knife to scribe faint parallel lines on to the blank space to the side and below the fish letter. Take the edible pen and write words appropriate to your cake beginning with 'Once upon a time', using the scribed lines as a guide **(G)** – there is lots of scope to personalize your story.

Tower

1. Thickly roll out the grey modelling paste and cut a triangle for the roof and place on the top right-hand corner of the cake. Smooth and straighten all the cut edges. Cover a small area under the roof with thinly rolled black modelling paste.

2. Take some of the pale-brown modelling paste and roughly knead in some brown paste colour to make marbled paste. Roll the paste into balls of different sizes and place under the roof and around the black paste to form the tower and window. Straighten the tower edges using a smoother then add a strip of grey between the tower and roof to neaten.

Trees and bushes

Take some of the green sugarpaste and model into rough tree and bush shapes. Take a pan scourer and press it firmly into the soft paste to give an interesting texture **(H)**. Attach on top of the cake to the side and base of the tower.

Unicorn

Roll out some white modelling paste between the narrow spacers. Press the unicorn cutter into the paste to emboss, and then cut around the embossed shape with a craft knife (**I**). (You can roll the paste thinner so the cutter cuts all the way through, but the unicorn will look a little flatter.)

Thatched cottage

1. Roll out some brown modelling paste and emboss with the mini-brick embosser. Cut out a 5 x 2.5cm (2 x 1in) rectangle. Place on the cake under the lettering, and then remove a door and two windows. Replace the door with modelling paste of another colour.

2. Make the roof by cutting some pale-brown paste into shape and texturing it with a cutting wheel. Add a chimney pot.

Rose stems

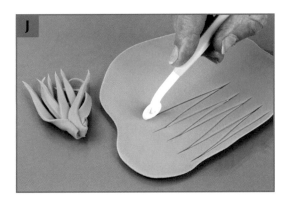

Soften some brown modelling paste by adding some white vegetable fat and boiled water until the paste has the consistency of chewing gum. Place in a sugar shaper with the small round disc and squeeze out lengths over the lower left-hand corner of the left-hand page. Arrange to look like a tangle of stems.

Reeds

Thinly roll out some green modelling paste and, using a cutting wheel, cut strips of reeds (**J**). Roll up the strips and place in a clump below the unicorn.

Rock and path

Make reddish-brown and marbled-grey modelling paste by roughly mixing in appropriate colours to modelling paste and use to make the path area leading from the reeds, and the rock.

Further details

1. Using appropriate cutters and coloured pastes cut out and attach to the cake the following: penguins, cat, teddies, bat, birds, moon, sun, and rose leaves and flowers.

2. Colour the royal icing brown, place in the piping bag with the no. 0 tube and pipe rose thorns on to the visible rose stems. Then add brown dots to the eyes of the unicorn, cat and penguins.

Bookmark

Roll out the red modelling paste between the narrow spacers and cut into a 2 x 30cm (¾ x 12in) strip. Take the star cutter and emboss stars on to the strip. Mark a line 2cm (¾in) in from one short end then repeatedly cut to this with a small pair of scissors to make a fringe. Place on the cake over the join between the pages.

Children

1. For the boy, roll a 1.5cm (⅝in) wide ball of black modelling paste and cut into two. Roll each half into a ball and then cone (**K**). Flatten the smaller end of each cone to form shoes and place on the board at the top right-hand corner of the book, flattened ends together.

2. Take a 2.5cm (1in) ball of purple modelling paste and roll into a 3.5cm (1⅜in) sausage. Cut most of the way down the length of the sausage to form two legs. Smooth to remove the ridges and place on top of the shoes.

3. For the body, take a 2.5cm (1in) ball of red modelling paste, elongate and flatten slightly then cut arms and smooth away the ridges. Make holes in the ends of the arms with the handle of a paintbrush and place on top of the body. Add hands, following the instructions on page 16, and arrange in place.

4. Place a sugar stick through the neck and down through the body and place the prepared head in position. Add hair using the sugar shaper fitted with a mesh disc.

5. Model the girl as for the boy but make her slightly taller with differently styled and coloured hair.

Painting

Dilute a selection of paste colours in clear spirit and paint over the added details to brighten and highlight the texture (**L**). Add small black dots over the eyes piped earlier. Add snowflake lustre dust to the unicorn, roses and moon, and finally mix some gold dust with confectioners' glaze and carefully paint over the embossed stars of the bookmark.

Short Cuts
* Omit the painting stages.
* When carving don't carve the spine area and leave the cake whole.
* Add less detail.
* Reduce the number of cutters used.

Imaginative Lettering

This cake has countless possible variations and can be easily personalized by adding letters. These can be piped, embossed, cut from modelling paste using letter cutters or, as this variation shows, made from plant, animal and fish cutters. Try experimenting to see what you can create. You can also get inspiration from the variety of illustrated alphabets available on the Internet.

The Frog Prince

*S*itting on a lily pad, The Frog Prince, wearing his golden crown, waits for the princess to repay him for fetching her golden ball by giving him a kiss. Only then can the witch's spell be broken so that he can regain his human form. Create this delightful cake for any child who loves the story or frogs in general. Although the cake may look complicated, by using the templates provided you will be able to achieve a recognizable and lifelike form for the frog.

Materials
23cm (9in) square Madeira cake made with 8 eggs (see page 10)
25g (1oz) pastillage
paste colours: golden brown, light green, bright green, deep yellow
edible gold lustre dust
white vegetable fat (shortening)
sugar glue
sugarpaste (rolled fondant): 600g (1lb 5oz) pale green, 200g (7oz) yellow, 800g (1¾lb) green
1 quantity buttercream
modelling paste: 25g (1oz) yellow, 15g (½oz) black, 15g (½oz) white
small amount of white royal icing
clear spirit, such as gin or vodka
confectioners' glaze
piping gel (from cake-decorating suppliers)

Equipment
thin card or stiff paper to make former
narrow spacers made from 1.5mm (1⁄16in) thick card
30cm (12in) board
cabbage leaf
glass-headed dressmakers' pins
waxed paper
Dresden tool
piping bag(s) with nos 1, 2 and 3 piping tubes (tips)
paintbrushes: large, small, flat-headed
2cm (¾in) circle cutter
stippling brush
green ribbon and non-toxic glue stick
pan of simmering water

PREPARATION

Preparing the cake for freezing
Level the cake and place in the freezer overnight.

Pastillage crown
1. Make the crown's former from thin card by drawing around the base and sides of the crown template and across the top of the points. Cut it out and stick the two sides together to make a cone.

2. Colour the pastillage golden to match your gold lustre dust. Smear white vegetable fat on your work board and roll out the pastillage between the narrow spacers. Place the crown template on the paste and cut out the crown. Stick the two sides together with sugar glue and place inside the former to dry.

Covering the board
Roll out the pale-green sugarpaste and use it to cover the board. Press the veins on the underside of the cabbage leaf gently into the soft paste. Repeat this, repositioning the veins to create a radial pattern to give the illusion of a lily pad (see picture **C**). Leave to dry.

STAGE 1

Carving the cake
1. Place the frog template on top of the frozen cake, and secure with glass-headed pins. With a large knife, cut vertically through the cake around the template **(A)**. Mark the hind legs by cutting along the lines of the template. Reduce the height of the hind legs to 3.5cm (1⅜in) and the front legs to 3cm (1⅛in). Spread buttercream on the top front of the body and add one of the hind-leg offcuts to form the head.

Tip

It is worth spending time getting the frog shape correct, remove a little cake at a time until you are happy with the appearance.

2. Using the profile template as a guide, carve the body of the frog from the middle of the back down to the tail; shape the head and remove a wedge from the front. Curve all the cut edges of the body to give a rounded appearance.

3. Shape the front legs by carving from the body down to a height of 1cm (⅜in) and rounding all the edges. For the back legs, mark the leg lines on the template on to the cake. Accentuate these lines by removing a small wedge of cake, then gradually reduce the height of the legs from the knees to 1cm (⅜in) at the feet, and taper down from the knee to the tail, then curve all the cut edges.

4. Slightly cut away around the base of the cake to give a more rounded appearance.

Covering the cake

1. Place the cake on waxed paper and cover the front and half of the inside of the front legs with buttercream. Roll out the yellow sugarpaste, cut one edge straight and place the paste over the buttercreamed cake with the straight edge at the base. Cut the paste to fit the front of the cake. Then, with a finger, flatten the cut edge.

2. Take a Dresden tool and indent a few wrinkles in the frog's skin. Spread buttercream over the head and back of the frog, omitting the legs (**B**). Roll out the green sugarpaste and use to cover this area. Cut the paste away from the base of the cake and around the legs. Flatten the cut edge around the tops of the legs with a finger.

3. For the mouth, carefully cut the paste so it slightly overlaps the yellow sugarpaste at the front and then round the cut edge with a finger so that the top lip stands proud of the yellow front.

4. Cover the two front legs with buttercream, then green sugarpaste. Trim away the excess paste and blend the joins with a finger. Roll four toes for each foot and blend the joins. Indent the paste with a Dresden tool to form wrinkles in the skin across the front of each foot. Cover the back legs, and indent the recesses with a Dresden tool. Add toes as above.

Adding eyes

Roll two 2.5cm (1in) balls of yellow modelling paste and attach to either side of the top of the frog's head. Leave to dry.

Cup Cakes

Cover each cup cake with a disc of green sugarpaste. Thinly roll out some gold modelling paste and cut out crowns using the cup cake template; sugar-glue in position. Pipe on decorative detail using royal icing and leave to dry. Brush white vegetable fat over each crown and dust with gold lustre dust.

Decorating the crown

Remove the dried crown from its former. Colour the royal icing to match the crown. Place a small amount of icing in a piping bag then using the suggested tubes, pipe decoration on to the crown. Leave to dry.

Painting the board

Slightly dilute some light-green paste colour in clear spirit, load a large paintbrush and paint the board to highlight the veining (**C**).

STAGE 2

Decorating the cake

1. Thinly roll out some black and white modelling paste and cut two 2cm (¾in) circles from the black paste and two small circles using a piping tube from the white (**D**). Attach the black circles to the centre of the yellow eyeballs for pupils and the white to one side of the black for light spots. Take some green sugarpaste and roll into a sausage. Taper both ends, and place under the eyeball. Roll a longer shape for the top of the eye. Sugar-glue in position. Create wrinkles and nostrils by indenting with a Dresden tool.

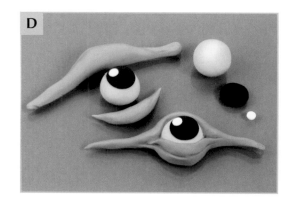

2. Add three thin lines of sugarpaste along the frog's back (**E**), and then add flattened elongated balls of sugarpaste randomly over the frog's body.

Gilding the crown

Brush white fat over the crown and dust with edible gold lustre dust.

Painting the cake

Separately mix some green and deep-yellow paste colour with clear spirit. Take a flat-headed brush and paint over the front of the frog with vertical strokes of yellow paste colour. Then stipple over the remaining cake with green. Leave to dry.

STAGE 3

Assembling the cake

To make the frog look wet, stipple over the entire cake with confectioners' glaze. Then carefully place the cake on the prepared board, sugar-glue the crown in position and add a ribbon around the edge of the board. Make a few water droplets by placing some piping gel in a bowl over a pan of simmering water until the gel has softened and is lump-free. Remove it from the heat, dip a paintbrush into the gel and carefully touch the board to create water droplets (**F**). Repeat as desired.

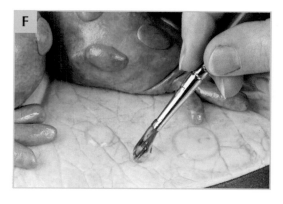

Splendid Crown

Make the crown more elaborate by piping on a different pattern and using graduated dragées (sugar balls). Alternatively, dust it an alternative colour; there are many edible dust colours available, so the choice is yours.

Jolly Pirate

*T*he world of the pirate is full of exciting adventures and swashbuckling deeds that appeal to the imagination of young children. Several of the storybook pirates are comical characters, and our lovable rogue fits the bill perfectly. The Jolly Pirate sits astride a barrel as he chuckles heartily waving a cutlass and a Jolly Roger flag. There are several elements to this cake that require care, but full details as well as a carving sketch and templates will assist you in achieving an impressive result.

Materials

sugarpaste (rolled fondant): 1kg (2¼lb) white, 800g (1¾lb) light brown

paste colours: selection of blues, black, brown

chocolate cake made with 10 eggs and baked in a 18 x 30cm (7 x 12in) rectangular tin (pan) (a multisized cake pan is ideal) and a 7.5cm (3in) round tin (such as a food can) (see page 10)

1 quantity chocolate buttercream

50g (2oz) pastillage

white vegetable fat (shortening)

clear spirit, such as gin or vodka

modelling paste: 150g (5oz) black, 15g (½oz) yellow, 15g (½oz) orange, 150g (5oz) flesh, 125g (4½oz) red, 15g (½oz) white, 50g (2oz) brown

sugar glue

Equipment

30 x 25.5cm (12 x 10in) oval cake board

spacers: narrow spacers made from 1.5mm (⅟₁₆in) thick card, 4mm (⅛in) spacers

cutting wheel

craft knife

pieces of foam

sugar shaper with medium round and mesh discs

circle cutters: 10cm (4in), 1.5cm (⅝in), 7mm (⁵⁄₁₆in) (use piping tube/tip),

waxed paper

straightedge, such as a ruler

scissors

paintbrush and large-headed paintbrush

ball tool

glass-headed dressmakers' pins

1.5cm (⅝in) square cutter

dowel

oval cutters: 3.25cm (1¼in), 2.75cm (1⅟₁₆in)

cocktail stick (toothpick)

Dresden tool

sea-green ribbon and non-toxic glue stick

PREPARATION

Covering the board

Take 700g (1½lb) of white sugarpaste and colour it in various of shades of blue (**A**). Roughly knead these colours together then cut the paste in half to reveal the resulting marbled pattern. Place the two halves next to each other, cut-side uppermost, and carefully rub the join closed. Roll out the paste and use to cover the board. Trim, then leave to dry.

Tip

When colouring the blue paste, save time by mixing three different blues, then taking small portions of each and kneeding them together to create a range of blues that blend.

A

Preparing the cake for freezing

1. Level the small round cake to a height of 6.5cm (2½in).

2. Level the rectangular cake. Cut the cake in half to make two 15 x 18cm (6 x 7in) cakes. Spread a thin layer of buttercream over one half and stack the other on top, then cut the cake to a height of 11.5cm (4½in). Freeze overnight.

B

Cutlass and flagpole

1. Colour 25g (1oz) of pastillage grey and roll out between the narrow spacers. Place the cutlass template on top and cut around the outline with a cutting wheel (**B**); remove the notches with a craft knife. Place on foam to dry.

Tip

An airing cupboard is an excellent place to dry pastillage.

2. Colour 25g (1oz) pastillage light brown and soften by adding a little white vegetable fat and a drop of water. Place in a sugar shaper with the round disc and squeeze out a 20cm (8in) length. Dry on foam. (Alternatively, a wooden barbecue skewer makes a sturdy flagpole.)

STAGE 1

Carving the cake

1. Place the frozen stacked cake on its end. Take a 10cm (4in) circle cutter and press into the end of the cake so that it overlaps the edge of the cake by 2cm (¾in) (see sketch). Repeat on the other end. Mark the centre of the top. Refer to the indented circles and mark the long sides halfway along in line with the widest part of the circles approximately 4cm (1½in) up from the base.

C

2. Carve the cake into a cylinder shape, by curving the edges of the cake between the markers, as shown on the sketch. Next, shape the cake down from the centre of the barrel to the marked circle on the end to form a barrel shape (**C**).

3. Curve the top edge of the small round cake with a knife then take a slice away from one side to form the front of the pirate.

Covering the barrel cake

1. Place the cake on waxed paper. Spread a thin layer of buttercream over the two ends of the barrel. Roll out some light-brown sugarpaste, cut one side straight and place on one end of the barrel with the straight edge flush with the base. Cut the paste flush with the sides of the barrel (**D**). Repeat for the other end. With a straightedge, indent the surface of the paste with lines 2cm (¾in) apart. Add the wood-grain texture with a craft knife (**E**).

Tip

Allow yourself time to get the carving right – if the structure of the cake is correct the rest tends to fall into place!

2. Add two thinly rolled out, 2cm (¾in) wide strips of sugarpaste at right angles to the planks. Cut to size, and add a wood-grain texture as before.

Cup Cakes

Warm some white modelling paste and place a marble-sized ball in the head of a parrot mould (DP). Firmly press the paste into the mould and then release it. Paint the parrot's head with your choice of paste colours diluted in clear spirit, and leave to dry. Cover each cup cake with a disc of blue sugarpaste and top with a parrot's head. Alternatively, make coins, treasure chests or skull and crossbones.

3. Spread buttercream over the main body of the barrel. Cover with light-brown sugarpaste. Trim to fit at the base of the barrel, then use scissors to cut the paste at the ends so it overlaps by 1cm (⅜in). Use a straightedge to indent a line lengthways along the top of the barrel. Indent the other lines 2.5cm (1in) apart at the centre of the barrel and tapered to 1.5cm (⅝in) at the ends. Add the wood-grain pattern. Leave to dry.

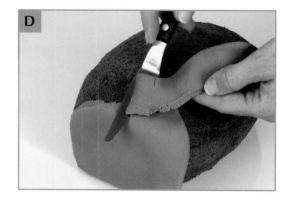

Covering the pirate cake

Place the small round cake on waxed paper and cover with buttercream. Cover with the remaining white sugarpaste. Trim the paste from the base and leave to dry.

STAGE 2

Trimming the barrel

Using a craft knife, remove a thin slice from the ends of each plank to flatten and neaten.

Painting the barrel

Dilute some brown paste colour with clear spirit and paint the barrel using a large-headed paintbrush. Leave for a few minutes then sweep a brush along the planks to emphasize the pattern.

STAGE 3

Position the barrel cake centrally on the board. Cut four 1cm (⅜in) wide strips from thinly rolled black modelling paste and wrap around the barrel for the rings.

Trousers

1. Roll out a long strip of black modelling paste 5cm (2in) wide between the 4mm (⅛in) spacers. Cut one long edge straight and wrap around the lower half of the pirate cake so that the straight edge forms the waistband. Cut to size at the back and blend the join closed. Tuck the excess paste underneath the cake for a rounded edge. Attach to the top of the barrel then round the top cut edge of the trousers with a finger.

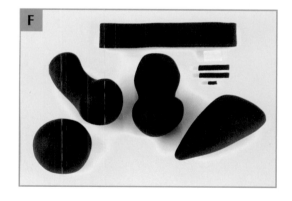

2. For the legs, roll two 2.5cm (1in) balls of black paste into cones. Cut the larger ends straight and attach to the cake.

Boots

Roll a 2.5cm (1in) ball from black modelling paste, mould to a bone shape **(F)**. Insert the larger end of a ball tool into the smaller end of the 'bone'. Cut a 5.5 x 1.25cm (2¼ x ½in) strip from thinly rolled black modelling paste. Wrap the strip around the indented ball and smooth the join. Sugar-glue the boot to the leg and support in position with a pin and a piece of card **(G)**. Add a buckle made from yellow and black modelling paste.

Belt

Paint sugar glue around the top of the trousers. Make a 5mm (³⁄₁₆in) wide belt from orange modelling paste and a buckle from yellow modelling paste using the square cutter; attach an orange strip and a small sausage of yellow, for the pin.

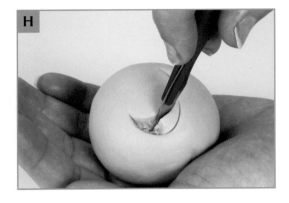

Head

1. Insert a dowel through the neck of the pirate to support the head. Take 125g (4½oz) of the flesh modelling paste and roll most of it into a ball. Hold the large oval cutter at an angle of 45 degrees and indent the top lip, then take the small oval cutter and indent the bottom lip. Remove some of the paste from inside the open mouth with a craft knife **(H)**. Indent the corners of the mouth with the small circle cutter. Model a nose from two small and one slightly larger balls of paste. Indent eyes with the end of a paintbrush. Place the head on top of the dowel.

2. Model a tongue from red modelling paste. Indent a line down the centre then attach inside the mouth. Add a tooth and tiny balls of white for eyes. Add pupils and white light spots. Use a cocktail stick to indent holes for whiskers.

Scarf and coat

1. Model the scarf from orange modelling paste **(I)**, attach to the neck then indent with a Dresden tool. Roll out the red modelling paste between the narrow spacers and cut into a 23 x 9cm (9 x 3½in) strip. Curve the top corners and drape around the shoulders of the pirate.

2. Add red lapels, using the template, to the front of the coat. Thinly roll out some yellow modelling paste and cut into thin strips. Paint sugar glue around the edges of the lapels and coat and trim with the yellow strips.

Arms

1. Roll 25g (1oz) of red modelling paste into a ball, then a sausage and then a bone shape **(J)**. Press a ball tool into one end and cut the other at 45 degrees. Repeat for the other arm.

2. Roll a 1.5cm (⅝in) ball of flesh modelling paste into a cone. Pinch the fatter end to flatten then, using scissors, cut out a small triangle to form the thumb. Make three cuts to form four fingers. Round the cut edges and insert into the arm. Repeat for the other hand.

3. Attach the arms to the cake. Place the cutlass in the right hand, wrapping the fingers around the handle, and support in position with foam. Place the flagpole in the left hand and support with foam **(K)**. Leave to dry.

Tip

If you are short of time or working in humid conditions, place the arms down by his sides.

Hat

Cut an out an oval of black modelling paste rolled between narrow spacers to fit the pirate's head. Glue in position. Cut a 14 x 2cm (5½ x ¾in) strip and remove a part circle from the centre of one long side using a 1.5cm (⅝in) circle cutter. Taper the strip from the two corners of the circle to the ends of the strip. Add yellow trim as for the coat, and then stick in place around the centre of the hat.

STAGE 4

Hair

Knead the brown modelling paste until warm. Add some white vegetable fat and boiled water to soften until it has the consistency of chewing gum. Place in the sugar shaper with the mesh disc. Paint sugar glue around the sides and back of the head. Squeeze out a 4cm (1½in) length of hair, remove it from the shaper with a Dresden tool, twist and squeeze both ends together and attach the loop to the back of the head. Continue adding loops to give a full head of hair **(L)**. Adjust the loops with a Dresden tool.

Finishing off

1. Add an orange modelling-paste handle to the cutlass.

2. Cut out a black flag from thin modelling paste and add a skull and crossbones modelled from white sugarpaste (see sketch). Wrap the flag around the top of the flagpole and leave to dry.

3. Attach a ribbon to the edge of the board.

Short Cuts

- ☠ Omit the cutlass and flag.
- ☠ Omit the painting stages.
- ☠ Change the pirate's expression.

Treasure Chest

All pirates have a hidden treasure chest somewhere, and this one is full of sweets (candies) to appeal to young children. Carve the cake into a chest shape rather than a barrel. Cover the lid and base separately then texture and paint. Place the base on an island made from soft light-brown sugar, decorate with a golden lock and, of course, sweets, and then place the lid in position.

King Arthur's Castle

*S*tories about the adventures of King Arthur and his knights of the round table have captivated *S*children for hundreds of years, and boys, especially, will love this version of Camelot, King Arthur's castle. It stands on a brightly decorated board with chequered corners and the knights' colourful shields set around the border, which can be easily personalized. This is a fairly simple cake for a beginner to make – just give yourself time to complete the intricate border.

Materials

sugarpaste (rolled fondant): 800g (1¾lb) black,
   675g (1lb 7oz) red, 2.4kg (5lb 4oz) warm grey
small amount of white pastillage
Madeira cake made with 10 eggs and divided
   between a 25.5 x 12.5cm (10 x 4⅞in) rectangular
   tin (pan) and 8 x 7.5cm (3in) diameter food cans
   (see page 10)
   or 4 store-bought family sized Madeira cakes
   and 4 jumbo Swiss (jelly) rolls, at least
   20cm (8in) long
1 quantity buttercream
5ml (1 tsp) gum tragacanth
sugar glue
modelling paste: 50g (2oz) red, 15g (½oz) brown,
   25g (1oz) black, 25g (1oz) white, 25g (1oz) blue,
   25g (1oz) yellow, 25g (1oz) orange, 25g (1oz)
   green

Equipment

35.5cm (14in) square cake board
4mm (⅛in) spacers
7.5cm (3in) diameter empty food can with
   both ends removed
stone-wall embosser (FMM)
circle cutters: 7.5cm (3in), 4.5cm (1¾in)
foam (undulated)
1cm (⅜in) square cutter
paintbrush
glass-headed dressmakers' pins, if necessary
craft knife
shield cutter (FMM set 3)
narrow spacers, made from card
zigzag cutter (FMM)
black ribbon and non-toxic glue stick

PREPARATION

Covering the board

1. Using a pencil, indent a line 5.5cm (2¼in) in from each side of the board to form a 24cm (9½in) central square. Roll out the black sugarpaste between the 4mm (⅛in) spacers and cover this square. With a straightedge and knife, trim to size using the indented lines as a guide.

2. Roll out a strip of red sugarpaste between the 4mm (⅛in) spacers. Cut one edge straight and place against one side of the black square. Trim the edges flush with the board. Repeat for all sides. Leave to dry.

Making the flagpoles

Roll the pastillage into four thin, uniform sausages. Leave to dry. (White candy sticks also make ideal flagpoles, if you prefer.)

Preparing the cake for freezing

Home-made: level the rectangular cake and remove the crusts. Cut in half to make two 12.5cm (4⅞in) square cakes. Spread a thin layer of buttercream over the top of one and stack the other on top. Level each cylindrical cake. Spread buttercream over the top of four and stack the remaining four on top, making four towers. Freeze. *Store-bought*: level the Madeira cakes, and stack them together as above. Carve to form a 12.5cm (4⅞in) cube. Freeze.

Carving the cake

Mark the frozen cube cake on each top edge 3cm (1⅛in) in from the corners. Use the food can as a cutter to remove the corners **(A)**. Remove crusts from the frozen tower cakes and level to a height of 20cm (8in). Cut store-bought Swiss rolls to a length of 20cm (8in).

Covering the cake

1. Cover the top of the castle with a thin layer of buttercream. Roll out some of the grey sugarpaste and place on top of the cake. Trim the paste flush with the sides of the cake (**B**).

2. Cover the sides of the cake with buttercream then roll out a strip of sugarpaste at least 20cm (8in) wide and 50cm (20in) long. Cut one long edge straight.

3. Carefully roll up the paste like a bandage and position it against the side of the cake with the cut edge at the base. Unroll the paste around the stacked cake, ensuring that the join in the paste will be in one of the corner recesses. Cut the sugarpaste to fit the circumference and rub the join closed. Trim the paste flush with the top of the cake.

4. Take the stone-wall embosser and emboss the sides and top of the cake by gently but firmly pressing it into the soft sugarpaste.

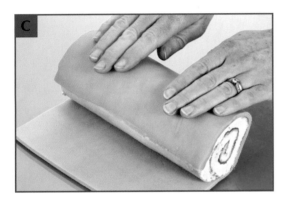

5. Carefully place the cake in the centre of the prepared board. Roll out a small amount of grey sugarpaste and cut out four circles using the 7.5cm (3in) cutter. Place these on one end of each tower using buttercream to secure them in place.

6. Cover one of the tower cakes with a thin layer of buttercream. Roll out some grey sugarpaste to at least 20 x 25.5cm (8 x 10in). Cut one of the longer edges straight, then place the buttercreamed cake on to the sugarpaste so that the uncovered end is flush with the cut edge. Roll the cake up in the sugarpaste and cut away the excess (**C**). Rub the join closed, and then trim the paste flush with the top of the cake.

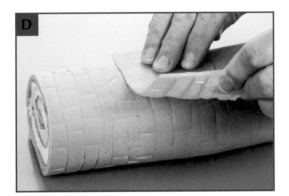

7. Emboss the tower (**D**), then position it in one of the corner recesses of the square cake, using sugar glue to secure. Repeat for the other three towers.

Preparing modelling paste

Add the gum tragacanth to 225g (8oz) of the remaining grey sugarpaste to create modelling paste. Leave to mature overnight.

The flags

Break the flagpoles into 10cm (4in) lengths. Thinly roll out the red modelling paste and cut out four flags using the flag template. Apply sugar glue to one end of each flagpole and wrap the wider end of the flag around to secure it, then top with a ball of black paste. Drape over curved foam to dry.

Cup Cakes

Cut out a disc of red sugarpaste to fit the top of each cup cake.
Decorate with shields as made for the cake.

Decorating the castle

1. Roll out a strip of grey modelling paste between the 4mm (⅛in) spacers. Cut into a 3.5cm (1⅜in) wide strip. Using the square cutter, remove squares along one long edge to create castellations **(E)** and then emboss the paste with the stone-wall embosser. Paint a line of sugar glue around the top of one tower and wrap the embossed paste around it. Cut to fit. Use clean glass-headed pins to help hold the paste in position while it dries. Repeat for the remaining towers, and then add castellations to the top edges of the castle.

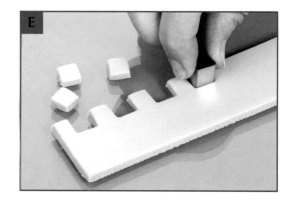

2. Roll out some more grey modelling paste, emboss and cut to fit the front of the castle to a height of 10cm (4in). Paint sugar glue around the edges and attach in place. With a craft knife remove a 7cm (2¾in) high arch. Add castellations to the top of the newly added section.

3. Cut out a door from brown modelling paste using the shield cutter and mark vertical door panels. Attach in place. Cut four 4.5cm (1¾in) circles from black modelling paste. Mark each into eight segments. Attach to the centre of the towers with sugar glue and insert the flags.

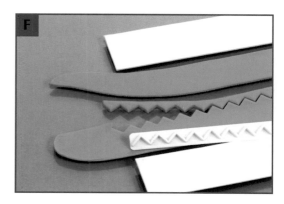

Adding windows and arrow slits

Thinly roll out some black modelling paste and cut thin strips for arrow slits and windows. Attach to the castle walls as desired.

Decorating the board

1. Roll out the white modelling paste between the narrow spacers, into a thin strip. Press a zigzag cutter into the paste. Create 1cm (⅜in) wide zigzag strips by cutting straight lines either side of the zigzag, and attach the strips to the edge of the black sugarpaste on the board. Make two more, then make four blue zigzag strips **(F)** and attach these to abut the white ones. Cut blue and white squares from the modelling paste to form a chequered pattern at the board's corners.

2. Roll out the remaining modelling pastes between the narrow spacers and cut out shields and decorations. Decorate as desired and attach to the board.

3. Add black and red trim along the zigzag strip and around the chequered board if desired. Attach a black ribbon around the edges of the board with a glue stick.

Fairytale Castle

This castle is easily adapted to suit little princesses. I have used cream sugarpaste for the walls and added a turret instead of castellations on the towers. To make the turret, cover a large ice-cream cone with pink sugarpaste and 'tile' it with pink and white modelling-paste hearts. Decorate with pearlized gold dragées.(sugar balls).

Noah's Ark

For animal-loving children you can't beat a Noah's Ark packed with animals of all sizes, shapes and colours. You can include your child's favourite animals, and you will find that many of the animals given in the instructions can be adapted to create other species. A brightly coloured embossed trim at the top of the hull adds to the impact of this splendid ark, bobbing on choppy waves. Give yourself plenty of time to fill the ark with your choice of creatures.

Materials

Madeira cake made with 9 eggs and divided between a 24 x 16.5cm (9½ x 6½in) oval ovenproof dish and a 15cm (6in) square tin (pan) (see page 10)
1 quantity buttercream
sugarpaste (rolled fondant): 1kg (2¼lb) green, 500g (1lb 2oz) turquoise blue, 600g (1lb 5oz) white
2.5ml (½ tsp) gum tragacanth
sugar glue
paste colours: bright green, dark blue, bright blue
clear spirit, such as gin or vodka
modelling paste: 100g (3½oz) orange, 25g (1oz) deep pink, 25g (1oz) bright blue, 100g (3½oz) yellow, 50g (2oz) red, 50g (2oz) grey, 25g (1oz) white, 25g (1oz) brown, 25g (1oz) black
white vegetable fat (shortening)
sugar sticks

Equipment

waxed paper
straightedge, such as a ruler or palette knife
35.5 x 30cm (14 x 12in) round cake board
spacers: 5mm (³⁄₁₆in) spacers, narrow spacers made from 1.5mm (¹⁄₁₆in) card
paintbrushes, including a flat-headed brush
stippling brush, such as a shaving brush
circle cutters: 4.25cm (1⅝in), 2.25cm (⅞in), 2cm (¾in)
scissors
2cm (¾in) square cutter
small embossers (HP)
zigzag cutter (FMM)
small round piping tube (tip)
sugar shaper with half-moon disc
ball tool
cocktail stick (toothpick)
sea-green ribbon and non-toxic glue stick

STAGE 1

Carving the cake

1. Cut the crust from the oval cake and level to a height of 6.5cm (2½in) **(A)**. Place on waxed paper. Cut the crust from the square cake and level to a height of 6.5cm (2½in). Cut the square cake in half and place one half on waxed paper. Cut the remaining cake, for the roof, to a height of 5cm (2in), then mark the centre lengthways along the top of the cake and carve from 5mm (³⁄₁₆in) either side of this line to the lower long edge.

2. On the short sides cut from 2.5cm (1in) in on the top to the lower short edge **(B)**. Spread a layer of buttercream over the top of the small rectangular cake and place the roof cake on top. Remember, if you have time, place the roof in the freezer before carving, because it is much easier to carve a frozen cake.

Covering the cake

1. Place the bowl cake upside-down on waxed paper. Cover with a thin layer of buttercream then rolled-out green sugarpaste (**C**). Take a straightedge and, holding it approximately 7mm (⁵⁄₁₆in) up from the waxed paper, press it into the sugarpaste and carefully turn the cake to indent a line all the way around the cake. Repeat at similar intervals over the hull of the ark (**D**).

2. Secure some waxed paper to a cake board or similar and place on top of the overturned ark. Turn the ark over. Next, cover the top of the hull with a thin layer of buttercream and then green sugarpaste. Cut the edges of the sugarpaste flush with the sides of the hull.

3. Spread a thin layer of buttercream over the small cake and cover each side separately with turquoise sugarpaste. Trim the sides to shape, and blend all joins.

Making modelling paste

Add the gum tragacanth to 100g (3½oz) of green sugarpaste trimming, and leave to mature, overnight if possible.

STAGE 2

Making the hull

Warm the green modelling paste and roll out between 5mm (³⁄₁₆in) spacers then cut into a 2cm (¾in) wide strip. Paint a line of sugar glue around the rim of the boat and then place one cut edge of the strip over the glue to make the side of the ark. Cut to size.

Painting the ark (optional)

1. Dilute some of the green paste colour in clear spirit and paint the hull of the ark in sweeping strokes with a flat-headed brush.

2. Separately dilute the blue paste colours and stipple the dark blue followed by bright blue in lines around the top cake (**E**). Clean the brush and stipple over the edges of the painted areas with the clean, damp brush to blend the colour with the unpainted surface.

Tip

If you paint the ark, do allow time for the paint to dry before moving to stage 3.

Cup Cakes

Cover each cup cake with a disc of green sugarpaste. Thinly roll out modelling pastes in animal colours and cut out a selection of animals using animal cutters (FMM Safari Animal set). Attach three animals to each cake. Then dilute some paste colour in clear spirit and paint each animal to enhance its markings.

STAGE 3

Covering the cabin

1. Roll out the green modelling paste between narrow spacers and cut one edge straight. Paint sugar glue around the sides and top of one end of the cabin and position the modelling paste with the straight edge flush with the base. Trim the sides so they are flush with the carved cake and cut the top horizontal where the side meets the roof. Then indent parallel horizontal lines on to the paste with a straightedge at approximately 7mm (⁵⁄₁₆in) intervals.

2. Cut out an arch from the green paste to reveal the blue sugarpaste below, using a 4.25cm (1⁵⁄₈in) circle cutter to cut the curves. Repeat for the other end. Cover the remaining sides in the same manner, then create windows by removing four circles from each using a 2.25cm (⁷⁄₈in) circle cutter.

Covering the roof

Roll out the orange modelling paste between the narrow spacers. Paint sugar glue along the ridge. Place the paste over the roof then with scissors carefully cut the orange paste so it overlaps the sides slightly. Remove three 2cm (¾in) circles of paste from each side **(F)**.

Decorative band

1. Roll out some green, pink, orange, blue and yellow modelling paste between the narrow spacers. Cut out squares of each colour using the square cutter and emboss each colour with a different embosser **(G)**. Stick the squares in a band around the top of the ark.

Tip

If you don't have any embossers, you will find that buttons, piping tubes, straws, and so on, work just as well.

2. Roll out the red modelling paste between the narrow spacers, into a long, thin strip. Press a zigzag cutter into the paste and remove. Create 8mm (⁵⁄₁₆in) wide zigzag strips by cutting straight lines either side of the zigzag, and sugar-glue the strips to the lower edge of the decorative strip and around the lower edge of the roof. Make yellow zigzag strips and attach these below the red on the ark. Emboss each yellow triangle using a small round piping tube (see the main photograph on page 41 for this decorative detail).

3. Soften some red modelling paste with white vegetable fat and boiled water and place in the sugar shaper with the half-moon disc. Squeeze out a length and glue to the top rim of the ark **(H)**. Add a strip of red modelling paste to the top of the roof.

Tip

A sugar shaper is an excellent tool for adding decorative trim quickly and effortlessly, but if you don't have one then cut a thick strip of red paste instead.

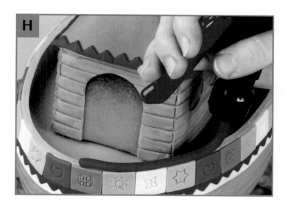

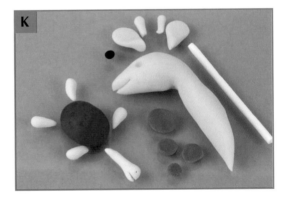

Covering the board

1. Place the ark centrally on the board and secure the cabin in place. Colour some of the blue sugarpaste trimmings a darker blue. Reserve 25g (1oz) of white sugarpaste then take a small amount of the remaining white, blue and green paste and roughly knead together to create marbled paste.

2. Roll the paste into a 2.5cm (1in) wide sausage and place on the cake board around one side of the base of the ark. Model the paste into wave shapes by using your fingers and a ball tool **(I)**. Continue adding sausages of marbled paste and shaping them into waves until the board is completely covered.

3. To make surf, take the reserved white sugarpaste and mix it with boiled water until it has a spreadable consistency. Using a paintbrush, add some surf to the tips of some of the waves then, with a damp flat-headed brush, smooth the white paste back over the top of the waves to give a more subtle effect **(J)**.

The animals

1. Model animals from modelling paste as shown (see pictures **K**, **L**, **M** and **N**). Each animal head is shaped firstly by rolling a ball of modelling paste of the correct colour and then shaping it. When a long muzzle is needed, roll the ball backwards and forwards in the palm of your hand exerting pressure on just one side to form a cone shape. To model the giraffe, elongate the ball and roll to form the neck **(K)**.

2. For the elephant, roll a ball of grey modelling paste into a cone and extend the thin end by rolling between your fingers to form the trunk **(L)**. The ears are flattened circles of paste. Make the tiger's stripes by using a cutting wheel to cut tapered strips of thin black modelling paste.

3. The animals can be easily varied to make others; for example, the giraffe can become the cow, the tiger can become a bear, and so on. Indent nostrils with a cocktail stick, cut mouths with a circle cutter held at an angle or with a small pair of scissors. Add eyes by indenting with a cocktail stick or adding small balls of black paste to the recesses made with the small end of a ball tool or glass-headed pin. Make the giraffe's and cow's spots from flattened balls of paste.

Tip

Use varying amounts of blue and green sugarpaste in the sausages to help the completed waves look more interesting.

Tip

Remember that the animals should be in pairs!

To finish

Attach the completed animals to the ark, using sugar sticks to help secure and support any long necks, such as the giraffe's and the ostrich's. Cut the necks or bodies of some of the animals at an angle to give them the appearance of leaning out of the doors and windows of the ark. You can add as many or as few animals as time allows. Attach a ribbon to the board.

Tip

Use small pieces of foam to support the animals in position while they dry.

Short Cuts
🐑 Omit painting.
🐑 Reduce the number of animals.
🐑 Simplify the decoration.
🐑 Make a calmer sea.

Favourite Animals

The ark is an ideal opportunity to include some of your child's favourite animals. Here are a few more to inspire you to be creative. You could also include some brightly coloured butterflies, amphibians, insects and birds.

Little Mermaid

*D*elight your child or teenager with this intricately modelled mermaid combing her hair as she rests on a shell-covered rock where delicate seaweed grows. The surface of the rock and fish-scale texture of the mermaid's tail add to the naturalistic appearance of the cake and are easy to achieve following the detailed instructions. Give yourself plenty of time to create the face and hands, and colour the eyes and hair the same as the person you are making the cake for.

Materials

modelling paste: 150g (5oz) flesh, 50g (2oz) cream, 25g (1oz) orange, 75g (3oz) sea green, 50g (2oz) golden brown, 25g (1oz) light green

paste colours: for the face, plus brown, orange, cream, black

edible dusts: skin tone/pink for cheeks, white, green lustre, blue lustre, green, brown

sugar stick or uncooked dried spaghetti

clear spirit, such as gin or vodka

Madeira cake made with 6 eggs and baked in a 3 litre (5¼ pint) ovenproof bowl or in a 20cm (8in) round tin (pan) and carved to shape (see page 10)

½ quantity buttercream

sugarpaste (rolled fondant): 1.6kg (3½lb) white, 100g (3½oz) blue

sugar glue

pearlized ivory dragée (sugar ball)

white vegetable fat (shortening)

confectioners' glaze

piping gel (from cake-decorating suppliers)

Equipment

large adult head mould (HP)

paintbrushes, including no. 00

shell moulds or shells and material to make your own

starfish mould (DP – large seashore)

28cm (11in) cake round board

Dresden tool

stippling brush

selection of round piping tubes (tips)

narrow spacers made from 1.5mm (1⁄16in) thick card

cutting wheel

foam

sugar shaper with mesh disc

4cm (1½in) circle cutter

ceramic veining tool (HP) or cocktail stick (toothpick)

sea-green ribbon and non-toxic glue stick

Making the body and head

Make the mermaid's body, using the body template, and head as described in the Face and Figure Modelling section on pages 14–16, but do not make the two diagonal cuts on her lower body. Insert the sugar stick or spaghetti into the head so it will rest slightly forward and to one side once it is placed on the neck. Cut the neck at a slight angle to one side. Leave to dry thoroughly.

Shells and starfish

1. Knead the cream modelling paste until warm. Roll a small ball and press it into a shell mould and then release. As the size of the ball used determines the size of the shell, for small shells press the paste into the tip of a large mould **(A)**.

2. Make an assortment of small shells, remembering to keep them in proportion with the mermaid; if you make large shells she will look tiny next to them.

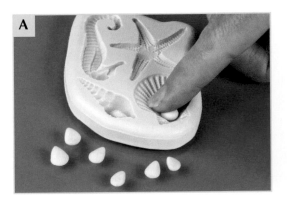

3. Make a starfish by rolling five thin sausages of orange modelling paste. Place one sausage in each arm of the starfish mould and press down firmly. Cut off any excess paste from the back of the mould and release.

4. Separately dilute some brown, orange and cream paste colours in clear spirit then add some edible white dust to all but the orange. Paint over the starfish with the orange then paint the shells to highlight their texture and shape. Leave to dry.

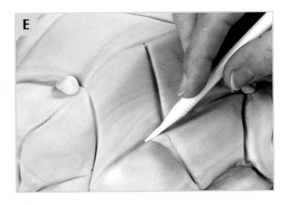

STAGE 1

Covering the cake

1. Level the bowl cake and remove the crusts **(B)**. Place the levelled surface in the centre of the cake board. Cover the cake with a thin layer of buttercream. Take 300g (11oz) of white sugarpaste and add pieces to the cake to disguise the dome shape and make it look more rocky **(C)**.

2. Colour all but a marble-sized ball of the remaining white sugarpaste a variety of shades of brown and grey **(D)**. Roughly knead these together then cut the paste in half to reveal the marbled pattern inside. Place the two halves next to each other, cut-side uppermost, and rub the join closed. Roll out the paste and use to cover the cake.

Texturing the cake

To form the rocks, take the sharper end of a Dresden tool and press and drag it through the paste along and across the lines of the marbling **(E)**. Roll small balls of sugarpaste and shape into pebbles. Place these randomly in some of the rock crevices.

Tip

To make the marbled pattern look more interesting, cover the cake in sections by cutting the marbled paste into pieces and place them on the cake at angles to one another. Blend all the joins closed with the heat from your fingers.

Adding the water

Cut away small sections of the marbled sugarpaste on the edge of the cake board. Roll out some blue sugarpaste and cut shapes to fit the exposed board areas. Place the paste shapes in position on the board. Ease the paste in to fit and then trim the edges flush with the edge of the board.

Painting the cake

1. If you have time, allow the sugarpaste to dry before painting. Dilute some brown paste colour in clear spirit and paint over the sugarpaste to intensify the colour of the rocks and give them a more realistic appearance **(F)**. Then take a dry stippling brush and stipple over the painted surface to remove the brushstrokes and give a mottled effect.

2. Add a darker colour to the rock recesses to exaggerate their depth, and stipple on some black and white patches to the top of the rocks. Leave to dry.

STAGE 2

Mermaid's tail

1. Roll the sea-green modelling paste into a sausage the width of the mermaid's body, then taper it to a rounded point and cut to a length of 15cm (6in). Place the tail in position on the cake but do not stick. Place the dried body of the mermaid on top of the tail and press it into the soft paste and then remove it.

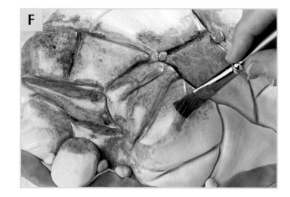

2. Place the indented tail in the palm of your hand and, taking the largest piping tube and holding it at 45 degrees, press half-circles around the top of the body indentation. Add a couple more layers under the first, and then change to a slightly smaller tube and repeat. Continue reducing the tube size at intervals until you reach the end of the tail. Cut the end of the tail in two with scissors. Attach the tail in position on the cake.

3. Roll out the remaining paste between narrow spacers and cut out the tail fin using the template and a cutting wheel. Texture the fin by repeatedly rolling the cutting wheel over the paste, being careful not to cut all the way through **(G)**. Note: the texturing spreads the paste and gives the tail fin a more realistic appearance and movement.

Tip

Add one or two small pieces of foam under the edges of the fin to hold it slightly away from the rock until the paste dries.

4. Place between the two halves of the cut tail section and sugar-glue in place. Lightly dust over the tail with blue and green lustre dusts.

Cup cakes

Cover each cup cake with a disc of blue sugarpaste. Make and paint starfish as described on page 46. Position a starfish in the centre of each cake.

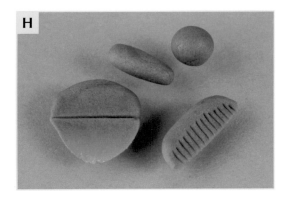

Assembling the mermaid

1. Glue the body to the tail. Paint the face (see page 15). Roll a small pea-sized ball of flesh modelling paste and stick to the top of the neck, place the head on top and blend away any visible paste from the ball with a Dresden tool.

2. Place two shells of the same size on her chest and place a pearlized ivory dragée between.

3. To make the comb, take a pea-sized ball of sea-green paste, roll it into a small sausage, flatten one side and cut this flattened side straight to form the comb shape. Cut into the flattened side with a craft knife to form teeth (**H**).

4. Make the arms following the instructions on page 16 and attach to the body blending the join of the right arm into the body with a Dresden tool and placing the comb in her right hand. Prop up the arms with pieces of foam so she looks as if she's combing her hair (**I**). Leave to dry thoroughly.

Tip

Only attempt to prop up the arms if weather conditions are dry – if it is wet and humid the arms will gradually sag once the supports are taken away, so it is probably advisable to place them down by her side or in her lap instead.

STAGE 3

Mermaid's hair

1. Knead the golden-brown modelling paste until warm then add some white vegetable fat, to stop it getting sticky, and some boiled water to soften the paste. Keep adding a combination of white vegetable fat and boiled water until the paste has the consistency of chewing gum. Place the softened paste in the sugar shaper with the mesh disc. Paint sugar glue over the top of her head.

2. Squeeze out a length of hair, remove it from the shaper with a Dresden tool and attach to the back of the head. Continue adding more hair until the head is completely covered. Style the hair as desired, making sure that it looks as if she is combing it. Neaten any stray hairs by cutting them with a small pair of scissors.

Seaweed

1. To make the fan-shaped seaweed, thinly roll out some light-green modelling paste and cut out 4cm (1½in) circles (**J**). Cut the circles into segments and texture each by rolling over the paste with a ceramic veining tool or cocktail stick. Dust with green and brown dusts and arrange on the rocks in rosettes of three or more (**K**).

2. For the long seaweed, cut out long leaf shapes from thinly rolled light-green modelling paste with a cutting wheel (see picture **J**). Texture one side by rolling the ceramic veining tool or cocktail stick over it, and then texture the second side leaving a central vein. Dust with green dust and attach to the rocks. Add a few strands of green using the sugar shaper, if desired.

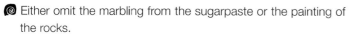

Finishing off

Randomly stick shells and starfish to the rocks. Then paint confectioners' glaze over the water and base of the rocks before adding piping gel over this area to give a watery effect. Make surf by mixing the reserved white sugarpaste with water until it has the consistency of thick paint and painting small amounts on top of the gel. Finally, add a ribbon around the edge of the board.

Short Cuts

- Either omit the marbling from the sugarpaste or the painting of the rocks.
- Place the mermaid's arms by her side, so drying time is not required.
- Omit the piping gel water and surf.
- Simplify the seaweed or rocks.

Happy Mermaid
Simplify the modelling required by making this cheeky mermaid. For her face instructions see page 16.

Arabian Nights

Create the luxurious palace where the beautiful and talented princess Sheherazade related imaginative and tantalizing stories over a thousand and one nights to her fearful husband, who had vowed to take a new bride every night and behead her in the morning. This opulent palace, with its gold-topped towers, is definitely for those who love the mystic Middle East or for children who have enjoyed the stories of Aladdin and Ali Baba, just two of Sheherazade's tales.

Materials
Madeira cake made with 9 eggs divided between
  a 15cm (6in) round tin (pan) and a 20 x 15cm
  (8 x 6in) rectangular tin (see page 10).
for the rock sugar: 500g (1lb 2oz) granulated
  sugar, 125ml (4fl oz) water, 25g (1oz) royal icing
1 quantity buttercream
sugarpaste (rolled fondant): 1.5kg (3lb 5oz) white,
  500g (1lb 2oz) blue
gold and turquoise dragées (sugar balls)
2 x 15cm (6in) sugar sticks
5ml (1 tsp) gum tragacanth, plus a pinch
golden-brown paste colour
sugar glue
white vegetable fat (shortening)
edible gold lustre dust
confectioners' glaze
edible snowflake lustre dust
small amount royal icing

Equipment
sugar thermometer
cutters: circle cutters: 9cm (3½in), 5cm (2in),
  3.5cm (1⅜in), 1.5cm (⅝in), 1cm (⅜in); narrow
  petal cutters; 4cm (1½in) star cutter
waxed paper
28cm (11in) round cake board
spacers: narrow spacers made from 1.5mm (1/16in)
  thick card, 4mm (⅛in) spacers
palette knife
craft knife
small star embosser
Dresden tool
barbecue skewer
sugar shaper with small round disc
paintbrushes
piping bag with no. 1 piping tube (tip)
sea-green and gold ribbon and non-toxic glue stick

PREPARATION

Cutting and freezing the cake
Level the round cake. Cut the rectangular cake as indicated on the cutting diagram, but do not shape the towers. Level the depth of tower 1 to 5cm (2in) and the depth of tower 2 to 3.5cm (1⅜in). Place all the cakes in the freezer overnight.

Making the rock sugar
1. Line a large ovenproof bowl with foil. Place the granulated sugar and water in a heavy pan and heat gently until the sugar has dissolved, stirring occasionally.

2. Bring to the boil and continue boiling until the syrup reaches 138°C (280°F), removing any scum from the surface of the syrup but without stirring. To prevent sugar crystals forming above the line of the sugar, run a little water down the sides of the pan using a pastry brush; this is important because once the crystals begin to form or the syrup is stirred the sugar will crystallize before the syrup has boiled for long enough.

3. Quickly remove the pan from the heat and place the base briefly in a bowl of cold water to stop the cooking process. Do not leave long enough for the syrup to cool.

4. Immediately stir in the royal icing, and then pour into the prepared bowl and allow to cool. Mixing the cold royal icing with the hot sugar creates steam, which puffs up the sugar and creates the rock-like texture of the sugar.

Tip
If you do not have a multisized pan use a 20cm (8in) square tin and use the 10-egg recipe instead.

A

B

Tip

Don't worry too much about neat joins, as most of them will be covered by decoration.

STAGE 1

Carving the cake

1. Remove the crusts from the round cake, then take a 5cm (2in) circle cutter and remove approximately a third of a 5cm (2in) circle from the edge of the cake to enable tower 1 to slot into the base of the palace (**A**). Place the cake centrally on the cake board.

2. Remove the corners of towers 1–4 to create cylinders. Shape the tops of towers 1 and 2 as shown on the diagram. Cut the height of tower 2 to 12cm (4¾in) and towers 3 and 4 to 7cm (2¾in).

Tip

If it's warm, the cake defrosts quickly, so remove each piece of cake from the freezer when you are ready to work on it. It is also easier to cover the cakes with the buttercream when they are not fully thawed.

3. Level cake 6 and attach with buttercream to one side of the top of the round cake. Trim away the top corners of the cake to give a rounded appearance (see picture **A**).

4. Make a template of the top dome cake and place on one face of cake 5. Cut vertically around the template then repeat the process on the next face. Remove the corners of the shape to create a rounded dome. Place on waxed paper.

5. If necessary, adjust the cut of the cakes to ensure that they all fit together easily.

STAGE 2

Covering the cake

1. Cover tower 1 with a thin layer of buttercream. Roll out some white sugarpaste to cover the sides, with a little extra height. Cut one of the longer edges straight. Place the buttercreamed cake on to the sugarpaste so that the base of the cake is flush with a cut edge. Roll the cake up in the sugarpaste (**B**) and cut away the excess. Rub the join closed then gather the paste up over the dome and cut away the excess. Repeat for tower 2. Cut the sugarpaste flush with the top for towers 3 and 4, and finish each with a circle of sugarpaste.

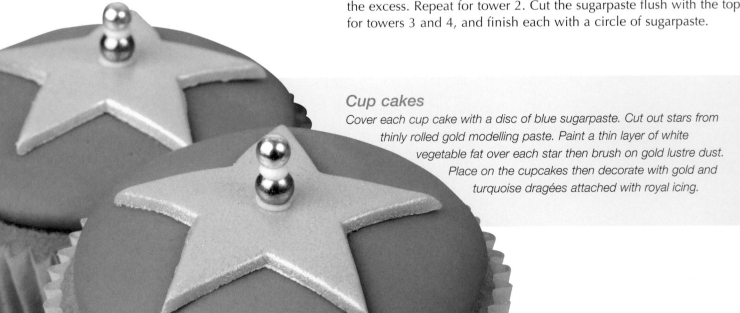

Cup cakes

Cover each cup cake with a disc of blue sugarpaste. Cut out stars from thinly rolled gold modelling paste. Paint a thin layer of white vegetable fat over each star then brush on gold lustre dust. Place on the cupcakes then decorate with gold and turquoise dragées attached with royal icing.

2. Cover the top dome cake 5 with buttercream. Roll out some white sugarpaste into a strip 15cm (6in) high and 25.5cm (10in) long. Cut one long edge straight and wrap the paste around the cake with the straight edge at the base. Ease in the fullness, cut away the excess paste and blend the join closed. Stroke the sugarpaste at the top into a point.

3. Add some sugarpaste to the base of cake 6 to give the palace a rounded appearance. Add some to the base of the round cake to create a base for the rock sugar **(C)**. Cover all but the sides of the base cake with buttercream. Roll out some white sugarpaste and place over the cake, ease in the fullness, and smooth. Cut the paste flush with the sides of the base cake.

4. Cover the sides of the base cake with buttercream. Roll out white sugarpaste into a long strip and wrap around the sides of the base cake. Trim flush with the top of the cake and blend the joins closed.

Assembling the cake
Place the top dome in position and attach a row of gold dragées around all but the front section of the base of the cake to hide the join with the main cake. Position the two larger towers. Place the smaller towers on top of the base cake and secure each one with a sugar stick.

Covering the board
Roll out some blue sugarpaste and cut into strips. Place the strips around the board and blend the joins closed with your finger. Texture the paste by firmly pressing into the soft paste and then stroking it to create wave patterns.

Adding rock sugar
Break the prepared rock sugar into pieces by tapping it gently with a wooden implement. Add to the sides of the cake and gently press them into the soft paste **(D)**.

Making modelling paste
1. Take 225g (8oz) of white sugarpaste and add 5ml (1 tsp) gum tragacanth to make modelling paste. Colour 175g (6oz) a light golden colour, to match the edible gold lustre dust to be used in stage 3. Add a pinch of gum tragacanth to 25g (1oz) of blue sugarpaste. Leave the modelling paste to mature.

2. Allow the sugarpaste to dry before moving on to stage 3.

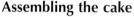

STAGE 3

Top dome
Roll out some golden modelling paste between the narrow spacers into a 15 x 25cm (6 x 9⅞in) strip. Paint sugar glue around the base and top of the dome. Wrap the paste around the dome with the join at the back. Ease the paste to the shape of the cake and cut away the excess at the back and top. Smooth the top of the dome into a point with your fingers and cut the lower edge straight. Cut a thin strip of blue modelling paste and wrap around the base of the golden dome. Indent vertical lines with a palette knife.

Tip

When covering the dome with modelling paste, you may find it easier to apply it in sections, say a quarter at a time.

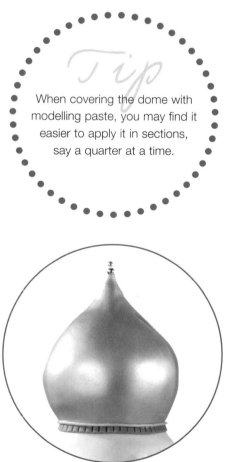

Windows

Thinly roll out the blue modelling paste and cut out windows using narrow petal cutters. Attach to the cake using sugar glue.

Ornamentation

1. Make a template of the stepped ornament. Roll out the white modelling paste between 4mm (⅛in) spacers, and cut around the template on top of the paste using a craft knife **(E)**. Attach eight around the front and back top edges of the base cake.

2. Using the two smallest circle cutters cut out three circles of each size from the 4mm (⅛in) thick modelling paste. Cut each in half and arrange the halves of the larger circle, straight-side down, at the base of the top dome cake, as a continuation of the row of gold dragées. Next, stick the curved side of the smaller halves on top of the larger half circles and top each with a small triangle of paste.

Blue-topped tower (tower 1)

1. Thinly roll out the blue modelling paste and cut out a 9cm (3½in) circle. Cut into the centre and remove an eighth of the circle. Attach to the top of the tower so that the join is at the back. Top with a large star cut from thinly rolled gold paste.

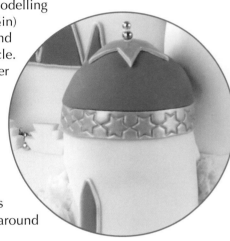

2. Cut a 1.3cm (½in) wide strip from thinly rolled gold modelling paste and emboss with small stars **(F)**. Attach around the edge of the blue dome.

Onion-domed tower (tower 2)

Warm 50g (2oz) of gold modelling paste and roll it into a ball, then a cone. Take a Dresden tool and firmly indent vertical lines from the base to the tip **(G)**. Press a finger into the base of the dome and push out the paste to widen its circumference at the base. Place on tower 2.

Slender towers (towers 3 and 4)

1. Cut strips from thinly rolled gold modelling paste and wrap around the top of each slender tower cake to cover the join in the white sugarpaste. Warm some white modelling paste and roll into a 1.75cm (¾in) wide sausage. Cut into two 5cm (2in) lengths. Make a hole through the length of each with a barbecue skewer and then carefully place over the protruding sugar sticks, and glue in place.

2. Roll out some gold modelling paste between the 4mm (⅛in) spacers and cut two 3.5cm (1⅜in) circles. Place discs on top of the towers. Then roll a 1.5cm (⅝in) wide white sausage of modelling paste and cut into 3.5cm (1⅜in) lengths. Attach to the top of the gold discs. Top each tower with small cones of gold modelling paste.

Trim

Soften some gold modelling paste by adding a little white vegetable fat and a few drops of boiled water until the paste has the consistency of chewing gum. Place the softened paste into a sugar shaper with the small round disc and squeeze out lengths. Place these around each of the windows, around the top of the blue strip on the top dome and above the gold strips on the slender towers.

Door

Roll out some gold modelling paste between narrow spacers and cut out a tall arch to fit the space between the slender towers. Indent a line down the centre and attach in place.

Adding gold

Mix some edible gold lustre dust with some confectioners' glaze, and paint over all the gold-coloured modelling paste (**H**).

Finishing off

1. Dust over the cake with snowflake lustre dust, then attach the onion dome to its tower.

2. Paint sugar glue over the area in front of the door and arrange gold dragées to fill the space (**I**). Sprinkle a few dragées over the rocks and the lower ornamentation.

3. Stack the gold and turquoise dragées on top of the towers secured by piped royal icing.

4. Put some softened white modelling paste in the sugar shaper. Squeeze out four short lengths and place around the base and top of the highest section of the slender towers.

5. Finally, attach a ribbon around the edge of the board using non-toxic glue.

Short Cuts
- Reduce the number of towers.
- Omit the rock sugar and the lustre dusts.

Brightly Coloured Palace
If you require a less sophisticated palace, altering the colours and using sweets (candies) for decoration can easily change the design. Children always love sweets on their cakes, so choose their favourite colours and varieties for a fun alternative.

Spooky Ghost

*M*ost children love to be scared by grisly ghost stories set somewhere remote, dark and mysterious. All the better for small children if the ghost is rather comical. This friendly ghost, rattling his chains as he drifts over a castle floor, will appeal to small and older children. A chocolate cake baked in a tiffin tin or pudding basin forms the base, and the ghost is covered with sugarpaste, moulded over sugarpaste padding to create a flowing, ghostly outline.

Materials

sugarpaste (rolled fondant): 500g (1lb 2oz) grey,
   150g (5oz) black, 1.25kg (2¾lb) white
black paste colour
chocolate cake made with 4 eggs, baked in a
   medium tiffin tin (pan), 16cm wide x 13cm high
   (6¼in wide x 5in high) or a 1 litre (1¾ pint)
   pudding basin (see page 10)
½ quantity chocolate buttercream
modelling paste: 25g (1oz) red, 25g (1oz) white,
   50g (2oz) black
sugar glue
50g (2oz) grey pastillage
white vegetable fat (shortening)

Equipment

25.5cm (10in) (side-to-side) hexagonal
   cake board
pan scourer
paintbrush
kitchen paper
black ribbon and non-toxic glue stick
craft knife
large round piping tube (tip), such as no. 18
small piece of foam
ball tool
1.5cm (⅝in) circle cutter
small scissors
sugar shaper with medium round disc

Covering the board

1. Roll out the grey sugarpaste and use to cover the centre of the board. Place the cake tin or pudding basin, in which the cake was cooked, upside down in the centre of the covered cake board and cut around it.

2. Remove the paste from around the circle and roughly knead in some black paste colour to produce a marbled paste. Roll out the paste and cut it into rectangles of different sizes. Arrange these rectangles in roughly parallel lines on the uncovered sections of the board leaving a slight gap between each piece.

3. To give the effect of stone slabs, flatten some of the rectangles slightly with your finger so that their edges do not look too uniform. Texture the stones slightly by pressing a pan scourer into the soft paste, and then cut them flush with the edge of the board. Leave to dry.

Tip
To create a realistic stone pattern, cut the kneaded marbled paste in half to reveal an intricate pattern before rolling it out.

4. Mix some of the leftover grey sugarpaste with boiled water so the paste has the consistency of thick paint. Darken it slightly with some black paste colour, and, with a loaded paintbrush, place the paste between the stones **(A)**.

A

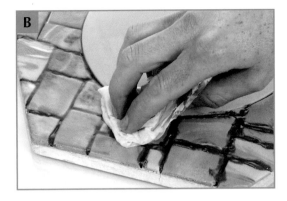

5. Dampen some kitchen paper and wipe it over the surface of the stones to help spread the paste into the grooves and to give the stones more colour and texture **(B)**. Leave to dry. Secure the ribbon to the sides of the cake board with a glue stick.

STAGE 1

Covering the cake

1. Level the cake and place the levelled surface in the centre of the covered cake board. Spread a thin layer of buttercream over the cake to help the sugarpaste stick.

2. Roll out the black sugarpaste and use to cover the front of the cake, where the mouth will be. Then take some of the white sugarpaste and create the shape of the ghost by adding lumps and bumps to give fullness to the body **(C)**.

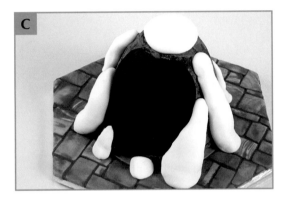

3. Roll out the remaining white sugarpaste and use to cover the cake. Even out the folds, moulding them to the shapes beneath, and trim to an appropriate shape.

The mouth

1. With a craft knife, carefully cut out a mouth shape from the white sugarpaste on the front of the cake to reveal the black paste underneath.

2. Take the piping tube and, holding it at an angle of 45 degrees, indent each corner of the mouth.

The tongue

1. Knead the red modelling paste and roll out to a thickness of approximately 5mm (³⁄₁₆in). Cut a 4.5 x 2.5cm (1¾ x 1in) rectangle and curve one end **(D)**. Smooth the cut edges except for the short, straight edge. Indent a line down the centre of the tongue, and then texture the surface with a pan scourer.

2. Smooth the texturing slightly and attach the straight edge to the lower lip of the mouth with sugar glue. Support in position with foam, and remove when dry.

The eyes

1. Knead the white modelling paste and roll two 2cm (¾in) wide balls. Indent eye sockets into the cake with a ball tool then stick the eyeballs in place and flatten slightly.

Cup Cakes

Cut out a disc of black sugarpaste to fit the top of each cup cake. Thinly roll out some orange and white modelling paste and, using Hallowe'en cutters (PC, FMM), cut out your choice of Hallowe'en characters and attach to the little cakes. Add Star Sprinkles (W) if you like.

2. Thinly roll out some black modelling paste and use the 1.5cm (⅝in) circle cutter to cut out two circles for pupils. Attach these to the eyeballs with sugar glue so the ghost looks cross-eyed, and add small white balls of modelling paste for light spots. Finally, stick 3.5cm- (1⅜in-) long sausages of black modelling paste at the back of the eyes.

The hands

1. Roll a 3.5cm (1⅜in) ball of black modelling paste and cut it in half. Roll one half into a ball, and then make a sausage shape that is thinner at the halfway point, to make a wrist; flatten one half slightly to form a hand **(E)**.

2. Take a pair of scissors and cut into the hand to form the thumb and fingers. Flatten each finger and smooth all the cut edges. Indent arm sockets into the cake with a ball tool then attach the arms in place with sugar glue. Leave to dry.

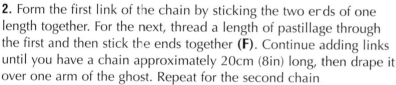

The chains

1. Soften the grey pastillage by adding a small pea-sized knob of white vegetable fat and few drops of boiled water. Place in the sugar shaper with the medium round disc and squeeze out a length of paste. Cut the pastillage into 5cm (2in) lengths. (Alternatively, you can roll the paste by hand.)

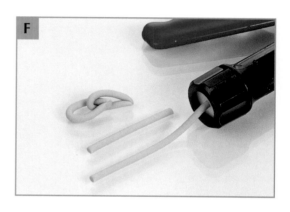

2. Form the first link of the chain by sticking the two ends of one length together. For the next, thread a length of pastillage through the first and then stick the ends together **(F)**. Continue adding links until you have a chain approximately 20cm (8in) long, then drape it over one arm of the ghost. Repeat for the second chain

Pumpkin Cake
Bake a 6-egg Madeira cake in a 15cm (6in) ball tin. Carve away small vertical sections to create the characteristic pumpkin shape. Cover the front with black sugarpaste, as for the ghost, and then cover the complete cake with pale orange-yellow sugarpaste. Cut out the pumpkin's face to reveal the black paste underneath, as you did for the ghost. Model a stalk and leave to dry. Stipple over the dried sugarpaste with orange paste colour diluted in clear spirit, such as gin or vodka, and leave to dry. Transfer the finished cake to a prepared cake board.

Cinderella's Slipper

*T*he ever-popular tale of Cinderella, with her dainty glass slipper, dates back to at least the
17th century and makes an inspirational theme for a special cake. You can create an elegant
sugar version of the slipper set on a 'satin' cushion, which will delight young and old alike. To
achieve the sumptuous effect, a chocolate cake is carefully carved to form the cushion and covered
with sugarpaste, and the slipper is moulded using pastillage.

Materials

20cm (8in) square chocolate cake made with
  9 eggs (see page 10)
sugarpaste (rolled fondant): 700g (1½lb) pink,
  1kg (2¼lb) purple
edible dusts: pink lustre, violet sparkle, white lustre
white vegetable fat (shortening)
50g (2oz) pastillage
sugar glue
½ quantity chocolate buttercream
violet paste colour
clear spirit, such as gin or vodka
royal icing
150g (5oz) white modelling paste
dragées (sugar balls): pink, ivory

Equipment

30cm (12in) round cake board
textured rolling pin (HP Watermark Taffeta Pin)
paintbrushes
large wedding-slipper mould (SS)
1.5mm (1⁄16in) spacers, made from card
cutting wheel
greaseproof paper
small scissors
glass-headed dressmakers' pins
waxed paper
stippling brush, such as a shaving brush
piping bag with nos 3 and 1.5 piping tubes (tips)
smoother
2.5cm (1in) heart cutter
sugar shaper with large rope disc
miniature heart cutter
pink ribbon and non-toxic glue stick

PREPARATION

Preparing the cake
Level the cake and freeze overnight, until firm (it is important to
freeze the cake before carving to prevent the corners of the cushion
falling off).

Covering the board
1. Roll out the pink sugarpaste and use to cover the cake board.
Texture the paste by taking a textured rolling pin, holding one end
in the centre of the board and rolling the other over the soft paste to
form a radial pattern and achieve a fabric effect (**A**).

2. Trim the edges flush with the edge of the board. Take a large-
headed paintbrush and lightly apply some pink lustre dust to add
sheen. Leave to dry.

Moulding the slipper
1. Brush white vegetable fat onto the
sole and heel sections of the shoe
mould. Roll a tapered sausage of
pastillage and place into one heel of
the mould. Ease the paste into shape
so that it is flush with the side of the
mould then trim it level with the sole
of the shoe.

Tip

The slipper is made in
two halves that will be
glued together.

2. Roll out some pastillage between the 1.5mm (¹⁄₁₆in) spacers on a well-greased board, and then cut out the sole by placing the template on the paste and cutting around it with a cutting wheel (**B**). (To prevent unnecessary handling and possibly stretching the paste, make sure the sole template is the correct way up for the half of the sole you wish to make.) Brush a little sugar glue on the top of the heel and carefully place the sole in the mould. Repeat for the second half of the shoe.

STAGE 1

Preparing the carving template
Cut a 20cm (8in) square from greaseproof paper or baking parchment. Fold it diagonally in half to make a triangle and fold in half twice more. Mark 2.5cm (1in) in from the outside edge on the shortest side and draw a smooth curve from the mark to the outer corner. Cut along the curve then open out the template (**C**).

Carving the cake
1. Place the carving template on top of the frozen cake and hold in place with glass-headed pins. With a large knife, cut vertically through the cake along the lines of the template (**D**). Remove pins.

2. Mark a horizontal line midway around the cake. Then create the rounded shape of the top of the cushion by carving from this line up to the centre (see carving sketch). Round off all the square edges (**E**). Turn the cake over and shape the underside of the cushion in the same way.

Covering the cake
1. Place the cake on waxed paper. Spread a thin layer of buttercream over the uppermost half of the cushion to fill any holes and help the sugarpaste stick.

Cup Cakes
Cut out a disc of white sugarpaste to fit the top of each cup cake. Add material drapes and decorated hearts as for the shoe, and dust with lustre dusts. Spread a thin layer of buttercream over the top of the cup cakes and place the decorated discs in place.

2. Roll out the purple sugarpaste and cover the top of the cushion, gently easing in the fullness. Trim the paste to the midway line. Turn the cake over and cover the second half in the same way. Carefully trim to size then rub the two edges together with your finger to make a neat seam. Smooth the cake as necessary. Leave to dry.

Assembling the slipper

When the pastillage is thoroughly dry, release the two halves of the shoe from the mould **(F)**. Mix a little pastillage with some boiled water to make a thick glue and use to stick the two dried halves of the slipper together. Leave to dry.

STAGE 2

Painting the cake

Mix some violet paste colour and violet sparkle dust with some clear spirit. Take a stippling brush, dip it in the colour, remove any excess liquid from the bristles then carefully stipple the cushion all over **(G)**. Start underneath the cushion: pull the cake to the edge of your work surface and hold the waxed paper down so that the brush can easily reach the underside of the cake.

Constructing the slipper

1. Place some royal icing in the piping bag with the no. 3 tube and pipe the icing into the gaps between the two halves of the moulded slipper. Smooth any excess away with a damp paintbrush.

2. Paint sugar glue over the sole of the slipper. Roll out some of the modelling paste between the 1.5mm (¹⁄₁₆in) spacers and drape it over the glued sole. Stroke the modelling-paste sole with a smoother to achieve a smooth, even finish. Trim the paste around the toe, flush with the underside of the instep and around the heel **(H)**.

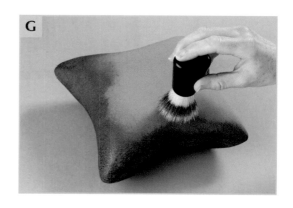

3. Draw the toe template on to a small sheet of waxed paper and place the slipper on top. Roll 25g (1oz) of white modelling paste into a ball and then form a cone. Place on the toe of the slipper and adjust the shape to fit the template. Shape the paste by smoothing and stroking it into position to create the toe former.

4. Using the spacers, roll out 25g (1oz) of modelling paste into a 4cm (1½in) wide strip. Cut out the slipper upper using the template and attach it to the sides of the instep and top of the toe former. Leave to dry.

5. Using the 2.5cm (1in) heart cutter, cut a heart from some of the modelling-paste trimmings and decorate with pink and ivory dragées.

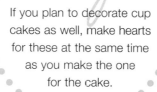

If you plan to decorate cup cakes as well, make hearts for these at the same time as you make the one for the cake.

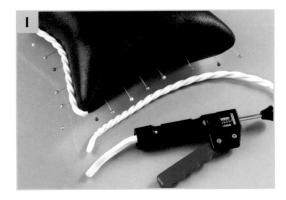

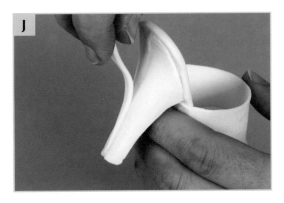

STAGE 3

Decorating the cushion

1. Soften some white modelling paste by adding a pea-sized knob of white vegetable fat and a few drops of boiled water. Place the softened paste into the sugar shaper with the large rope disc, and squeeze out a 25.5cm (10in) length. Twist the paste to form a rope, and then dust with pink and white lustre dusts.

2. Paint a line of sugar glue over the midway line on one side of the cake then insert pins just below the line to support the rope while the glue dries. Position the rope above the pins and cut to size **(I)**. Repeat for the other three sides.

Tip

Don't worry if you do not have a sugar shaper, add a row of hearts to cover the join in the cushion, or pipe a pattern in royal icing.

3. Remove all the pins. Roll a 1cm (⅜in) ball of paste, cut it into quarters and roll each quarter into a ball. Dust each ball with lustre dusts and stick one ball to each corner of the cushion.

Decorating the slipper

1. To neaten the heel, roll out some white modelling paste between the spacers, cut a strip and use to cover the inner heel. Then cut a thin triangle and place over the join at the back of the heel with the point at the base **(J)**.

2. Roll out some more modelling paste and texture it with the textured rolling pin. Cut into two 10 x 6cm (4 x 2⅜in) rectangles **(K)**. Fold over the short edges and make two pleats. Gather the pleats at one end of each strip and attach the gathered ends with sugar glue to the centre front of the shoe and the pleated sides to the outer edges. Wrap the paste around the back of the shoe, trimming to form a neat edge, and then cut the remaining paste flush with the sole of the shoe.

3. Attach a decorated heart to the centre with sugar glue. Cut a narrow, thin strip of modelling paste and wrap around the outside lower edge of the base of the toe to neaten. Using a miniature heart cutter, cut out hearts and attach them randomly to the shoe.

4. Place a small amount of white royal icing in the piping bag with the no. 1.5 tube, and pipe small dots around the top of the shoe's upper, the heart decoration, the base of the sole and the edges of the added heel strips.

5. Once the royal icing has set, brush the entire shoe with white vegetable fat, then cover the shoe with your choice of lustre dusts (**L**).

Tip

Experiment by adding one colour of lustre dust on top of another to create different effects (you can wipe off any mistakes, or practise first on leftover pieces of pastillage).

Assembling the cake

Place the cake centrally on the cake board and then secure the shoe in position with sugar glue. Attach the ribbon around the board with a glue stick and decorate with miniature modelling-paste hearts.

> **Short Cuts**
> - ❤ Leave the cushion unpainted.
> - ❤ Simplify the slipper: omit the pleats, and decorate the slipper with the large and tiny hearts painted with lustre dusts. Or add the pleats and single heart, omit the tiny hearts and finish with lustre dusts. The decorated slipper would also look effective without the lustre dusts.

Ballet Slippers

Using the templates, cut out the sole from thinly rolled white pastillage. Texture the surface (I used a PC embroidery grid embosser) and leave to dry. Add a rounded former for the toes. Cut out the two back sections of the slipper from thinly rolled peach modelling paste and glue in position with sugar glue, tucking the lower edges under the sole. Cut out the front of the shoe and attach to the back sections, tucking the paste under the sole. Leave to dry. Add a strip of paste to the top edge to neaten and run a stitching wheel along its edges. Position on the cake with a paste ribbon.

Teddy Tales

This adorable teddy bear sits on a picnic rug on the grass with a little cake waiting to be eaten, but he is gazing into the distance in the way that teddy bears always seem to do. Teddies have such a wide appeal that few people could resist this particularly lovable bear. His realistic fur is achieved by piping buttercream over the pre-carved cake. A carving diagram and full instructions make him an achievable project even if you have little experience of decorated cake-making.

Materials

700g (1½lb) green sugarpaste (rolled fondant)
225g (8oz) red modelling paste
Madeira cake made with 10 eggs and baked in a
  20cm (8in) round tin (pan), a 15cm (6in) round tin
  and a 10cm (4in) diameter ball tin (see page 10)
1½ quantity buttercream
paste colours: dark brown, golden brown
sweets (candies): 3 dark brown, 1 yellow
2 small biscuits (cookies), trimmed to the shape of
  the ear template

Equipment

28cm (11in) round cake board
2 different pan scourers
narrow spacers made from 1.5mm (1⁄16in)
  thick card
stitching wheel
dowel
circle cutters: 5.5cm (2¼in), 3.5cm (1⅜in)
palette knife
soft-bristled paintbrush
reusable piping bag with coupler, and piping tubes
  (tips): no. 4, medium star
petit four case
green ribbon and non-toxic glue stick

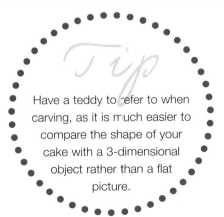

Tip

Have a teddy to refer to when carving, as it is much easier to compare the shape of your cake with a 3-dimensional object rather than a flat picture.

PREPARATION

Covering the board

1. Roll out the green sugarpaste and use to cover the cake board. Press a pan scourer repeatedly and firmly into the paste to create a grass texture **(A)**. Cut the paste flush with the edge of the board.

2. To make the rug, roll out most of the red modelling paste between the narrow spacers. Cut two edges straight, at right angles to each other. Mark a line 1.3cm (½in) in from each straight edge then cut this area into a fringe with a craft knife **(B)**. Texture the rug with a differently textured pan scourer, then mark with 2cm (¾in) squares using a stitching wheel and straightedge. Place the rug partially over the grass and trim away the excess flush with the edge of the board.

Preparing the cake for freezing

Level the two round cakes. If the ball cake has been cooked in two halves, level and stick together with buttercream. Place all three cakes in the freezer overnight.

STAGE 1

Carving the cake

1. Remove the cakes from the freezer as you need them. Place the carving template on top of the frozen 20cm (8in) cake and cut vertically around it with a large knife. Cut along the lines of the template to mark the legs and arms. Reduce the height of the legs to 5cm (2in), and then make a sloping cut 2cm (¾in) in from the end of the paws and further reduce the height of each leg to 3.5cm (1⅜in). Curve all the square edges of the legs to form oval paws and rounded legs up to the arms.

2. Place the carving template, minus the legs, on top of the frozen 15cm (6in) cake (do not worry that the arms overlap the edges), and carve vertically around the template. Spread a thin layer of buttercream over the top of the base cake and then place the round cake on top. Cut the cake to an overall height of 13.5cm (5¼in) and insert a dowel down through the centre of the cake to support the head **(C)**.

3. Using the 5.5cm (2¼in) circle cutter mark a circle on top of the cake with the dowel at its centre. Shape the back and front, but not the arms, by cutting down from this circle to approximately 4cm (1½in) up from the base and then cutting away a wedge of cake at the base to give the teddy a rounded appearance.

4. Create sloping shoulders by cutting down from the marked circle. Cut away 2.5cm (1in) from the length of the arms so that the paws rest on the sides of the legs. Mark the outline shape of each arm with your knife then cut away the excess cake, adjusting the shape of the back and front as necessary. Carve the arms to shape.

5. For the head, take the frozen ball cake and mark a round snout just below the midway line with the 3.5cm (1⅜in) circle cutter. Cut back from this by 2cm (¾in) from the top of the head, so that the snout protrudes from the face. Curve the snout to a cone with the point at the top. Flatten the top of the head slightly and curve the forehead and cheeks to give a more rounded appearance to the face. Place to one side.

Covering the cake
1. Colour a small amount of buttercream dark brown and, with a palette knife, spread some smoothly over the base of each paw **(D)**. Smooth the buttercream with a soft-bristled paintbrush that has been dipped into a pan of simmering water to heat it.

2. Colour the remaining buttercream golden brown. Cover the teddy with a thin layer to seal in the crumbs and place the cake in position on the prepared cake board.

3. Put some of the golden-brown buttercream into a reusable piping bag fitted with a no. 4 tube and, starting on one of the leg paws, repeatedly pipe short lengths around the paw. Pipe the next row to overlap the first row then continue until the leg is complete, gradually changing the direction of the piped lines to give the fur a natural look. Pipe the second leg, then, starting at the base of the teddy, pipe over his front and back bringing the icing up and over the neck edge **(E)**. Pipe the arms, starting from the paws.

Cup Cakes
Cover each cup cake with a disc of green sugarpaste. Texture with a pan scourer. Make square rugs with fringes from red modelling paste and place on the cakes. Knead some dairy fudge until warm and make teddies using a mould (DP Teddy Bears' Picnic). Place a teddy on each cup cake. Pipe eyes with a no. 1 tube and black buttercream.

4. Start piping the icing on to the base of the head. When two or three lines of icing are in place, position the head on top of the dowel so Teddy looks over to his right. Continue piping the icing up and over his head; change the direction of the fur on the front of the face so it all goes towards his snout (see the main picture).

5. Once the face is covered, place two brown sweets for eyes and one for a nose and add some more piping on top if necessary to blend the sweets into the icing. Then pipe two small dots on to the eyes.

6. For the ears, insert the biscuits into the top of the head **(F)**, cover the front of each with dark-brown buttercream, as for the paws, then pipe over the sides and back with golden-brown buttercream, as for the body.

Red Bow
Thinly roll out the red modelling paste between narrow spacers and cut into two 2cm (¾in) wide strips. To form the ribbon tails cut at an angle across one strip then cut again at the same angle to make a length of 10cm (4in) **(G)**. For the loops, cut the second strip to a length of 14cm (5½in). Mark the centre of the long strip and bring the ends of the strip in to make the loops. Place the loops on top of the tail strip and slightly squeeze the centre together. Wrap a 1cm (⅜in) strip around the centre. Attach under the chin of the teddy.

Tip

A ribbon cutter is a useful tool to cut the paste, as it saves time and ensures that the strips are a uniform width.

Miniature cup cake
Colour some of the remaining buttercream dark brown, place it in the piping bag and attach the star tube. Pipe icing into the petit four case, and top with a yellow sweet. Finally, attach the ribbon to the cake board.

Flower Teddy
Changing the scene in which the teddy sits can vary this cake simply. In this example the board has been covered in purple paste and simple flowers made from flower cutters have been added to the teddy's ear.

Flying Witch

*S*pells and magic are extremely popular with children, and this cheerful Flying Witch would make a perfect Hallowe'en cake or a birthday cake for a magic-loving child. The cake is straightforward to make, and templates and a cutting diagram are provided to help you, but it is always important to work through the modelling steps slowly to get the best results. Careful modelling of her flowing clothes and hair will give the impression that she really is flying.

Materials
50g (2oz) pastillage
dark-brown paste colour
modelling paste: 70g (2½oz) white, 25g (1oz)
    cream, 450g (1lb) pink, 225g (8oz) purple, 15g
    (½oz) red, 15g (½oz) orange, 25g (1oz) light
    green, 225g (8oz) black
white vegetable fat (shortening)
sugarpaste (rolled fondant): 800g (1¾lb) navy
    blue, 1kg (2¼lb) white, 100g (3½oz) light green
chocolate cake made with 4 eggs and baked in a
    medium tiffin tin (pan) 16cm wide x 13cm high
    (6¼in wide x 5in high), or cook two 15cm (6in)
    round cakes (6 eggs) and carve to shape (see
    page 10)
½ quantity chocolate buttercream
sugar glue
edible blue sparkle dust

Equipment
2 smoothers
foam
dowel
sugar shaper with large mesh disc
scissors
35.5 x 30cm (14 x 12in) oval cake board
star cutters (FMM)
narrow spacers made from 1.5mm (⅟₁₆in) card
waxed paper
kitchen paper
circle cutters: 1.5cm (⅝in), 10cm (4in)
embosser or patterned button
Dresden tool
cutting wheel (optional)
small circle cutter or piping tube (tip)
ball tool
blue ribbon and non-toxic glue stick

Pastillage broomstick
Colour the pastillage dark brown and roll some into a 1cm (⅜in) wide, 20cm (8in) long sausage. Use a smoother to do this to ensure that the sausage is even (**A**).

Cut it in half and leave to dry thoroughly on foam. An airing cupboard is an ideal place.

Head former
Take the white modelling paste and roll it into a ball. Insert a dowel, then place a smoother either side of the ball and squeeze slightly to make the head less rounded. Remove the dowel then leave the former to dry thoroughly.

Tip

As an alternative to white modelling paste, use a styrofoam ball as a head former, but be sure to tell the recipients that the head is not edible.

Completing the broomstick
1. Soften some pastillage by adding a small amount of white fat and boiled water. Place the softened paste in the sugar shaper with the large mesh disc and squeeze out a 10cm (4in) length and place on one end of one of the dried pastillage pieces. Flatten the paste where it joins the broomstick.

2. Repeat this process until the broomstick looks full. Then, holding the broomstick vertical, take a pair of scissors and trim the sticks shorter on the outside of the broom tapering to a rounded point in the centre **(B)**. Hang the broomstick up vertically and leave to dry.

Covering the board
Roll out the navy-blue sugarpaste and use to cover the board. Trim the paste flush with the sides of the board and emboss stars into the soft paste using the star cutters **(C)**. Roll out the cream modelling paste between the narrow spacers and, using the star cutters cut out some stars. Place the stars on top of the embossed ones and, with a finger, press down slightly on the points of each star to make them more rounded in appearance. Leave to dry.

Carving and covering the cake
Remove a 5cm (2in) high wedge from the lower front of the cake and remove a slice from the back at the top (see sketch). Place the cake on waxed paper and cover with chocolate buttercream **(D)**. Take 175g (6oz) of white sugarpaste and place at the back of the cake. Shape it to form the witch's skirt (see sketch). Roll out the remaining white sugarpaste and use to cover the cake completely. Trim flush with the base and leave to dry.

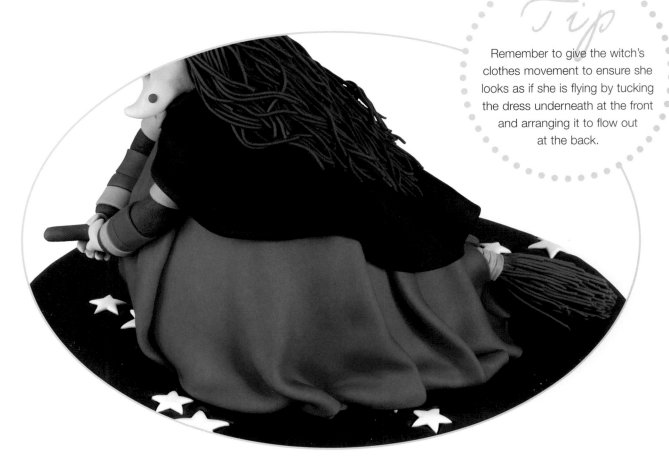

Tip

Remember to give the witch's clothes movement to ensure she looks as if she is flying by tucking the dress underneath at the front and arranging it to flow out at the back.

STAGE 2

Positioning the broomstick

1. Add some dark-brown paste colour to some of the remaining cream modelling paste and roll out. Cut the paste into thin strips and wrap around the top of the broomstick's twigs to form a binding.

2. Position the cake on the board, then insert the two sections of the broomstick into the cake, so that the witch will look as if she's flying.

Tip

Be careful to insert the pastillage sections so the broomstick looks straight.

Adding the dress

1. Roll out some of the pink modelling paste to a 15cm (6in) wide strip. Place one side up against the broomstick, and stick to the cake with sugar glue, gathering up the paste slightly to form lose pleats that fall from the witch's back down towards the broomstick. Allow the excess paste to fall in folds around the base of the witch, and then bring the paste around to the broomstick at the front. Cut the paste vertically down the mid-line. Repeat for the second side of the dress (**E**).

2. Trim off the excess paste from the witch's back and blend the cut edges into the white sugarpaste so that there are no hard lines.

Tip

You may find it easier to make the dress in stages by adding one piece on top of another and using the pleats to hide the joins.

Arms

1. Take 50g (2oz) of purple modelling paste and roll into two 11cm (4¼in) long sausages. Thinly roll out some red, orange and pink modelling paste and cut into strips (**F**). Wrap the strips around each sausage to form the multicoloured arms and attach with sugar glue. Make a hole in one end of each arm for the hand.

2. For the hands, take a 2cm (¾in) ball of green paste and roll into a cone (**G**). Pinch the fatter end to flatten it, and then take some scissors and cut out a small triangle to form the thumb. Make three cuts to form four fingers. Gently roll each finger until it is round, and insert it into the arm. Attach the arms to the cake with sugar glue, wrapping the hands around the broom handle.

3. Make the shoulders by rolling a 2cm (¾in) wide, 12.5cm (4⅞in) long white sugarpaste sausage from trimmings and attach it from the top of one arm around the back of the neck, leaving space for the head, to the top of the other arm.

Cloak

1. Insert a dowel through the top of the cake to support the head (see sketch). Add a 2cm (¾in) ball of green paste around the dowel for the neck.

2. Thinly roll out 225g (8oz) of black modelling paste and cut a cloak (see sketch). (You may need to adjust your measurements; make a template and check that it fits.) Gather up the two ends of the cloak and place around the shoulders of the witch. Take a piece of kitchen paper, fold in half then fold over 2.5cm (1in) and cut along the edge to make a support. Place the support under the cloak at the back to lift it off the cake so the witch looks as if she's flying. Add two more supports either side of the first then adjust the position of the cloak as required.

3. For the collar, roll out the black modelling paste into a strip. Fold the strip in half along its length, and then, with the fold making up one side, cut to a width of 2cm (¾in) and length of 17cm (6¾in). Next, taper the ends on the cut sides and attach around the top of the cloak to form a standing collar.

4. Add a clasp by cutting out a 1.5cm (⅝in) circle from orange modelling paste and embossing it with an embosser or button. Attach in position.

Head

1. Roll out the green sugarpaste and cover the dried head former. Roll two 2cm (¾in) green balls and model a chin and nose **(H)**. Place the modelled chin in position on the face and blend the joins with a combination of finger and Dresden tool. Rub firmly, and the join should almost disappear. Repeat the process for the nose.

2. Cut the mouth with a cutting wheel or Dresden tool then add corners by indenting a small circle cutter or piping tube at 45 degrees. Make the eye sockets with either a large-headed ball tool or a finger, and position the head on to the dowel so it rests comfortably on the cake. Roll some tiny pieces of red modelling paste and position on the nose and chin as spots.

Cup Cakes
Cover each cup cake with a disc of navy sugarpaste and dust with edible blue sparkle dust. Thinly roll out black modelling paste and cut out bats (bat cutters from PC, Halloween set). Position a bat and some Star Sprinkles (W) on each cake.

Hair

1. Soften some of the purple modelling paste by adding white vegetable fat and boiled water to make a soft paste the consistency of chewing gum. Place the softened paste into the sugar shaper together with a mesh disc. Place folded kitchen paper over the lower back of the witch's cloak to enable the hair to fly.

2. Squeeze out some lengths of paste and attach to the back of the head. Continue adding more sections of varying lengths until the head is completely covered. Arrange the hair with a Dresden tool so that it looks wavy and windblown **(I)**.

Eyes

Add a small pea-sized ball of cream modelling paste to each eye socket followed by black pupils and small light spots **(J)**.

Hat

Cut a 10cm (4in) circle from thinly rolled black modelling paste and place on top of the witch's head. Next roll 40g (1½oz) of black paste into a ball and then a cone and place on top of the hat. Create wrinkles in the hat with a Dresden tool and smooth into shape with a finger. Add a thin strip of pink modelling paste to hide the join and complete the hat **(K)**.

Finishing off

Once all the paste decorations have dried, remove all the kitchen-paper supports from the cake, brush sparkle dust over the blue areas of the board and attach a ribbon around the cake board.

Short Cuts

> ☽ Have a plain, blue board.
> ☽ Make the arms from a single colour.

Wizard

If you need a wizard rather than a witch, simply change the colour of the clothing and give him a long white beard and a receding hairline. You could also decorate his cloak with embossed stars or shapes of brightly coloured modelling paste, if you like.

Unicorn Myths

*M*agical unicorns are enchanting beasts that have appeared in stories throughout history. Young children, teenagers and adults, too, are fascinated by them, so this cake will have wide appeal. The cake is cut using a template to achieve the realistic shape, and the glossy, sleek coat of the leaping unicorn is created using buttercream that has been gently stroked using a paintbrush. If possible, refer to a toy or model horse while you sculpt the shape and smooth the buttercream.

Materials

1.7kg (3¾lb) white sugarpaste (rolled fondant)

sugar glue

modelling paste: 50g (2oz) bright blue

paste colours: bright blue, blue-purple, black, golden brown

clear spirit, such as gin or vodka

Madeira cake made with 9 eggs baked in a 25.5 x 23cm (10 x 9in) rectangular tin (pan) (a multisized cake pan is ideal) (see page 10)

buttercream: 1 quantity standard, 1 quantity white

edible snowflake lustre dust

small silver dragée (sugar ball)

Equipment

46 x 40.5cm (18 x 16in) rectangular cake board

narrow spacers made from 1.5mm (⅟₁₆in) thick card

various paintbrushes including large flat-headed paintbrush

greaseproof paper

glass-headed dressmakers' pins

craft knife/scriber

piping bag with coupler and piping tubes (tips) nos 17, 16, 4

palette knife

pan of simmering water

star cutter (FMM)

blue and silver ribbon and non-toxic glue stick

Tip

Use a 25.5cm (10in) square tin as an alternative but increase the batter to a 10-egg quantity.

PREPARATION

Covering the cake board

Roll out the white sugarpaste into a large rectangle and use to cover the board. Roll the bright-blue modelling paste into a long sausage and then roll it flat between the 1.5mm (⅟₁₆in) spacers. Cut four 4mm (⅛in) wide, strips from the paste and glue each strip to one edge of the board.

Colouring the board (flood-painting)

1. Slightly dilute some of the two blue paste colours separately with clear spirit. Take a large paintbrush and roughly paint each colour in sections over the board leaving some areas white **(A)**.

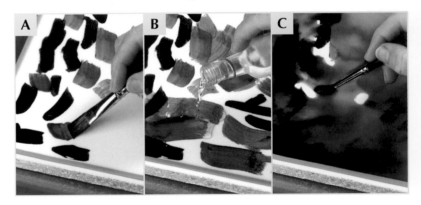

2. Carefully pour clear spirit or cooled boiled water over the partially painted surface **(B)**, then use a paintbrush to encourage the liquid into the corners and to cover the board entirely **(C)** (practise on a spare piece of sugarpaste first, if you like). The liquid will melt the surface of the paste so that the colours merge; this takes a few minutes. Leave undisturbed on a level surface to dry thoroughly.

Preparing the cake for freezing

Level the cake and cut in half lengthways to give two 13 x 23cm (5 x 9in) cakes. Freeze overnight.

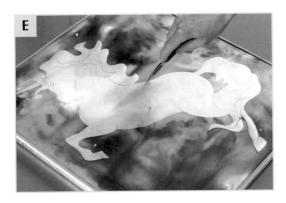

Carving the cake

1. Remove the crusts from the frozen cakes and spread buttercream over the end of one cake. Place the other cake up against the first to form an inverted 'L' (see page 102). Place the carving template on top and cut vertically around it. Mark the position of the legs and mane by cutting along the lines on the template. Remove the template.

2. Cut away the edge along the back to give a rounded appearance, and curve the edge between the legs. Shape the hind leg, and gradually reduce its height towards the knee. Reduce the height of the tail to 4cm (1½in) and curve all the edges. Shape the front leg and cut away the cake at the neck to reduce the height gradually to 2cm (¾in).

3. Shape the head (the buttercream will sculpt the detail). Add an offcut to the base of the mane. Shape and curve all the edges **(D)**.

Positioning the cake

Make a greaseproof-paper template of the unicorn and secure it in position on the prepared board with glass-headed pins. Take a craft knife and carefully mark the unicorn's outline on to the board **(E)**. Remove the template and place the cake within the outline.

Covering the neck and front

1. Half-fill a piping bag, fitted with the coupler, with white buttercream, and attach a no. 16 tube. Take a palette knife and thickly spread some white buttercream over the neck and front leg of the unicorn **(F)**. (To keep crumbs out of the buttercream avoid allowing the palette knife to come into direct contact with the cake.)

2. Pipe the foreleg, placing the buttercream between the scribed lines. Don't worry about the finish, as it will be smoothed.

Smoothing

Take a large flat-headed brush and dip it into the pan of simmering water to heat it; this prevents the buttercream sticking to the brush. Remove the excess water. Smooth the buttercream on the neck by making long, smooth strokes with the heated brush **(G)**. Continue smoothing the buttercream until it has all been smoothed. Change the direction of the brushstrokes to represent the body muscles.

Body

Cover the body, rump and thigh with white buttercream using a palette knife, and then pipe the lower hind leg between the scribed lines. Smooth as before.

Cup Cakes

Cover each cup cake with a disc of navy sugarpaste. Thinly roll out grey modelling paste and cut out horseshoes using a horseshoe cutter (FMM Celebration Tappits). Brush over each with white vegetable fat and then dust with edible silver lustre dust. Position a horseshoe and some Star Sprinkles (W) on each cake.

Head

1. Cover the head, using the scribed line as a guide to shape, and smooth. Add definition by piping extra buttercream where necessary to emphasize the cheeks, mouth and eye area. Smooth.

2. To create the eye, pipe a white dot for the eyeball using the no. 16 tube. Dilute some black paste colour in clear spirit and carefully paint over the eyeball. Change the tube to no. 4 and pipe eyelids. Smooth the side away from the eyeball. Pipe an eyebrow above the eye and smooth the buttercream away from the eye.

3. Create nostrils by making an indentation in the buttercream with a paintbrush and piping around this with a no. 4 before smoothing the outer edge. Create the mouth in the same fashion.

4. Pipe on an ear using a no. 16 tube then shape and smooth.

Horn

To achieve the spiral effect of the horn, pipe two lines across the horn with a no. 17 tube, then four with a no. 16 tube and finally three lines and the point with a no. 4 tube. Smooth to shape.

Mane, tail and hooves

1. Place some standard buttercream in a piping bag and fit the no. 16 tube into the coupler. Roughly cover the mane and tail using a palette knife, then add definition and movement by piping buttercream on top, using the scribed lines as a guide.

2. Smooth with a heated brush as before. Next, dilute some golden-brown paste colour in clear spirit and paint over the buttercream to add interest and depth. Pipe on the hooves (**H**) and paint (**I**).

Finishing off

1. Thickly roll out some white sugarpaste and cut out a few stars. Dust each with edible lustre dust and place randomly on the board.

2. Place a silver dragée in the corner of the eye for a light spot and attach a ribbon around the edge of the board.

3. If your unicorn is untidy around the edge where it meets the board, allow the buttercream to crust over then take a craft knife and scrape away any excess to give a neat edge.

A Special Horse

This cake design can easily be converted into a horse by omitting the horn and using buttercream of an appropriate colour. There is also plenty of space on the cake board to add a personalized message.

Woodland Fairy

This beautiful fairy sits on a tree stump surrounded by autumn leaves and toadstools. She would be suitable for any fairy-loving child, teenager or adult, and can be kept long after the cake has been eaten. She has a delightful natural-looking face, and can be made to look like the person for whom the cake is intended, simply by using the same colouring as for their eyes and hair. Figure modelling is an advanced skill, but precise instructions are given in the reference section.

Materials

sugarpaste (rolled fondant): 800g (1¾lb) mid-
   brown, 200g (7oz) cream, 400g (14oz) white
modelling paste: 150g (5oz) flesh, 25g (1oz)
   golden brown, 50g (2oz) cream
dried spaghetti
5ml/1 tsp powered gelatine
2.5ml (½ tsp) icing (confectioners') sugar
flower paste (from cake-decorating suppliers) or
   modelling paste: 50g (2oz) golden brown, 50g
   (2oz) mulberry, 15g (½oz) red
Madeira cake made with 4 eggs and baked in a 1
   litre (1¾ pint) pudding basin (see page 10)
½ quantity buttercream
paste colour: dark brown, golden brown, cream,
   colours for face
clear spirit, such as gin or vodka
sugar glue
edible dusts: copper lustre dust, pink/skin tone for
   cheeks, brown, red
confectioners' glaze
white vegetable fat (shortening)
piping gel (from cake-decorating suppliers)

Equipment

kitchen grater
pestle and mortar
large adult head mould (HP)
'U' tool (optional)
glass-headed dressmakers' pin (optional)
PVC sheet or plastic sleeve
pan of simmering water
cutters: leaf shapes, 2.5cm (1in) circle,
   2.3cm (¹⁵⁄₁₆in) long oval
leaf veiners
undulated foam and foam for support
acorn-cup mould (DP)
ball tool

equipment continued ...
25.5 cm (10in) round cake board
cutting wheel
craft knife
Dresden tool
foil, scrunched into a ball
pan scourer
paintbrushes, including large flat-headed
   paintbrush, no. 00 paintbrush
stippling brush, such as a shaving brush
17.5cm (6⅞in) plate
silk veining tool (HP), or textured rolling pin
no. 4 piping tube (tip)
mini-embosser
sugar shaper with mesh disc
small scissors
cocktail stick (toothpick)
brown ribbon and non-toxic glue stick

PREPARATION

Soil

1. Take a kitchen grater and grate some of the brown and cream sugarpaste. Leave to dry out completely.

2. Once hard, briefly grind the grated paste in a pestle and mortar to make small lumps (**A**).

Fairy body

Make the fairy body, using the body template, and head with flesh modelling paste as described in the Face and Figure Modelling section on page 14. Leave to dry thoroughly.

Wings

1. Make two sets of wing templates and place under a PVC sheet or inside a plastic sleeve. In a small bowl, soak the gelatine and icing sugar in 15ml (1 tbsp) of water. Dissolve over a pan of simmering water or in a microwave.

Tip

An airing cupboard is an excellent place to dry out models.

2. Working fairly quickly, take a teaspoon of this liquid and pour it carefully over one of the wing templates **(B)**. Do not worry if it spreads too far, as it can be trimmed later. Repeat for the other wing sections. Once the gelatine mixture begins to set, take a knife and cut radial lines through the wings. Allow the wings to set completely before removing.

Oak leaves and acorn cups

1. Thinly roll out the golden-brown flower paste and cut out a selection of leaves. Place each leaf in the double-sided veiner, and press together to vein. Place on an undulated surface and leave to dry.

Tip

If you do not have or cannot get hold of suitable veiners or moulds, it is easy to make your own by using a food-grade moulding medium such as Silicone Plastique, moulding gel or even pastillage.

2. Place a pea-sized ball of golden-brown flower paste in the acorn-cup mould. Press the paste into the mould with the larger end of the ball tool and circle the tool so the paste spreads up to the top of the mould **(C)**. Remove and repeat, then leave to dry.

STAGE 1

Covering the cake

1. Level the cake where it has risen, turn it over and level the top. Remove the remaining crust from the cake **(D)**. Place the cake in the centre of the cake board and cover with a thin layer of buttercream. Add pieces of sugarpaste to the sides of the cake to add form and bulk to the roots of the tree stump.

2. Roll out the cream sugarpaste and use to cover the top of the cake. Cut the paste flush with the sides of the cake. Indent the tree rings into the soft paste with a cutting wheel, starting at the outside and working in **(E)**. Next, take a craft knife and cut a few radial lines across the rings.

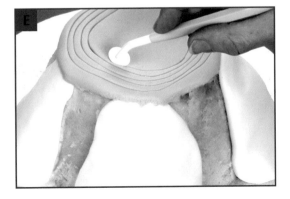

3. Roll out the brown sugarpaste into a 12.5cm (4⅞in) wide strip and wrap around the trunk. Cut the paste to fit the sides and smooth the join in the paste closed. Carefully cut the paste flush with the top of the cake and trim away the excess at the base. Texture the bark by making sweeping strokes through the soft paste with a Dresden tool, then press the scrunched ball of foil into the soft paste to add interesting, fairly deep texture.

Tip

Test your foil ball on a spare piece of sugarpaste first to see what textures it can produce.

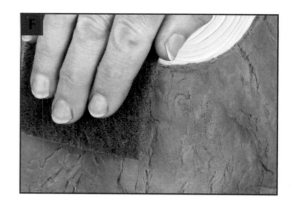

4. Soften the texture slightly by pressing a pan scourer over the textured paste **(F)**.

5. To cover the board, colour the sugarpaste trimmings with dark-brown paste colour and roll out into a long strip. Cut one edge straight and place on the board around the trunk with the straight edge abutting the cake. Trim away the excess and blend the join closed.

STAGE 2

Painting the stump
1. Separately dilute some golden-brown and dark-brown paste colours in clear spirit. With the flat-headed paintbrush paint the dark brown into the stump recesses, then paint over the remaining areas with golden brown using vertical sweeping strokes **(G)**. Blend the two colours by stippling over the wet painted surface with a dry stippling brush.

2. Dilute some cream paste colour in clear spirit and apply a wash to the tree rings. Leave to dry.

STAGE 3

Fairy legs
Model the legs using the figure template and instructions found on page 16. Attach the legs to the dried body and place in position. Do not stick to the cake yet. Bend the legs at the joints into a natural pose. Use foam as support, if necessary. Ensure the body is upright, and allow to become firm.

Cup Cakes
Make fairies using flesh-coloured modelling paste and a fairy mould (DP, baby fairy mould). Dilute some food colours and dust colours in clear spirit and paint the fairy. Leave to dry. Cover each cup cake with a disc of purple sugarpaste and secure a leaf, fairy and acorn on top.

STAGE 4

The fairy's skirt

1. Make a dress template by drawing around a 17.5cm (6⅞in) plate and cutting out the resulting circle. Fold the circle to find the centre, place the circle cutter in the centre, draw around it and cut out the circle. Cut into the centre from the outside and remove just over a third of the circle.

2. Roll out the mulberry flower paste on a well-greased work board. Place the template on top and cut around it with a cutting wheel. Remove small triangles from the edge of the skirt. Roll the silk veining tool or textured rolling pin firmly around the edges of the paste to frill and vein it (**H**), and then around the waist at the top.

> *Tip*
>
> There are many texturing tools and rolling pins available. Alternatively, use a cocktail stick, rolling it in the same way you would a veining tool but using variable pressure to create a pattern in the paste.

3. Paint a line of sugar glue around the waist of the fairy and wrap the skirt around so the join is at the back. Lift the body from the cake and tuck the paste under at the back so the fairy is sitting on her skirt. Arrange the folds of fabric so they fall naturally. Give movement to the edges of the skirt by turning up some of the points. Dust the skirt lightly with copper lustre dust.

The bodice

Thinly roll out the red flower paste into a strip, take a no. 4 piping tube and push up the paste on one long edge at regular intervals to create the undulated lower edge of the top. Paint a line of sugar glue down the sides of the body and in the middle of her back and wrap the red strip around the upper body so the undulations go around her waist and the join is at the back. Cut off the excess paste at the back join and ease in the fullness around her neck so that the paste sits neatly on her shoulders. Use a cutting wheel to style a neckline. Emboss a pattern around the neckline with a mini-embosser and finish off with a thinly rolled sausage of mulberry flower paste.

Inserting wings

Dust the edges of the dried gelatine wings with the copper dust and insert them through the red paste on the fairy's back. Support with foam, if necessary.

The arms

1. Model the arms following the instructions on page 16, and stick in place (**I**). Place some sugar glue inside each hand then wrap the hands around an acorn cup.

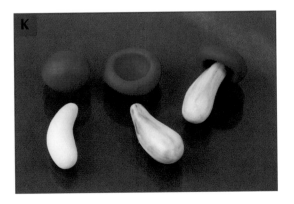

2. For the sleeves, roll out the mulberry flower paste on a well-greased board and cut out two ovals using the oval cutter (**J**). Frill as for the skirt, and attach to the top of each arm.

The head

Paint the face following the instructions on page 15, and add ears. Attach the head to the body using sugar glue. Soften some golden-brown modelling paste by adding a pea-sized knob of white vegetable fat and a few drops of water until it has the consistency of chewing gum. Place the softened paste inside the sugar shaper with a mesh disc. Paint sugar glue over the head. Squeeze out lengths of hair and attach them to the head starting at the back neckline and working up and around, finishing on the top of the head. Use a small pair of scissors to cut and style the hair.

Adding fungi and leaf litter

1. Using the cream modelling paste, roll some tapered sausages to make fungi stems and attach them around the tree stump. Insert small lengths of spaghetti into the taller ones for support. Dilute some golden-brown paste colour in clear spirit and paint streaks on each stem using vertical strokes.

2. Paint sugar glue over the covered cake board and sprinkle the prepared soil over. Dust the leaves with the edible dusts and arrange on top of the soil. Colour some of the remaining modelling paste brown, and roll acorns to fill some of the cups, indent a small hole in the top of each with a cocktail stick. Place on the board.

3. For the fungi caps, add some red flower-paste trimmings to brown modelling paste to create a reddish-brown paste. Roll a small ball, press the ball tool into the ball and place on top of one of the stems **(K)**, repeat for the remaining fungi.

Finishing touches

1. Heat a small amount of piping gel in a microwave or over a pan of simmering water then carefully place a few drops into the acorn cup that the fairy is holding **(L)**.

2. Finally, attach a ribbon around the board.

Short Cuts

- Omit the painting stage and the little details, such as the leaves and fungi.
- Change the fairy to a little girl or boy, so that there is no need to make the wings.

Cheerful Fairy
If modelling a lifelike face seems a bit too daunting, make a simple face following the instructions on page 16 and add your choice of hairstyle, perhaps to match the birthday girl's.

Dick Whittington's Cat

The 400-year-old legend of Dick Whittington, the poor orphan whose cat made his fortune, still has lots of appeal to children today. Indeed, cats are an all-time favourite and appear in many stories as well as being much-loved pets, so this contented and jolly cat is certain to be popular. The cake can also be modified to look like any favourite feline friend. This is quite a simple cake to make; take care when forming and attaching the pastillage whiskers, as they give the cake the perfect finish.

Materials

white vegetable fat (shortening)
sugarpaste (rolled fondant): 1.2kg (2lb 10oz) red, 800g (1¾lb) white
25g (1oz) pastillage
Madeira cake made with 9 eggs and baked in a 23 x 18cm (9 x 7in) rectangular tin (pan) and a 13 x 10cm (5in x 4in) tin (a multisized cake pan is ideal) (see page 10)
1 quantity buttercream
225g (8oz) black modelling paste
sugar glue

Equipment

40.5 x 35.5cm (16 x 14in) oval cake board
sugar shaper with small round and large round discs
waxed paper
dinner plate
Dresden tool
1.5mm (⅟₁₆in) spacers made from thick card
cutting wheel (optional)
thin paintbrush
cocktail stick (toothpick)
black ribbon and non-toxic glue stick

Tip
Improvise with the bakeware you have available and just increase the quantities slightly if using larger tins, for example, a 23cm (9in) square and a 13cm (5in) round tin.

PREPARATION

Covering the board

Cover your surface with white vegetable fat, then roll out the red sugarpaste and use to cover the board, trimming the sugarpaste flush with the edge. Place to one side to dry.

Whiskers

Soften the pastillage by adding some white vegetable fat, to stop the paste sticking, and cooled boiled water to soften it. Place the softened paste into the sugar shaper with the small round disc and squeeze out a 10cm (4in) length on to waxed paper around the edge of a dinner plate (**A**). Repeat at least five times, as you may need extras in case of breakages. Leave to dry. (It is not essential to have a sugar shaper, as you could roll the whiskers by hand. It is just a lot quicker and easier to make them if you do.)

Tip
Use white vegetable fat rather than icing sugar on your surface to prevent unwanted traces of white icing sugar.

Freezing the cake

Level the cakes and remove the crusts from their bases. Freeze the cakes overnight.

Carving the cake

1. Place the body template on top of the larger frozen cake and, with a knife, cut vertically through the cake along the lines of the template **(B)**. Mark the hind legs by cutting along the lines on the template, and then cut each leg to a height of 4cm (1½in) at the top sloping to 1.5cm (⅝in) at the feet.

2. Curve the body of the cake (see sketch) from the neck up to the front and down to the feet. Round all the cut edges on the legs and body. Remove a narrow wedge from the front of the body to define the front legs and cut away slightly at the base of the cake to give a more rounded appearance **(C)**.

3. Place the head template on to the remaining frozen cake and cut vertically around it. Carve away the top edge of the cake and cut away a small area at the base to create a rounded face.

Covering the cakes

1. Place both cakes on waxed paper. Spread a thin layer of buttercream over the cakes. Roll out the white sugarpaste and use to cover the body cake. Smooth the paste into shape with the palm of your hand then trim away the excess at the base.

2. Using the sharper end of a Dresden tool, indent a line between the front legs and around the hind legs. Cover the head cake with the white sugarpaste trimmings. Leave to dry.

Decorating the cake

1. Transfer the cakes to the covered cake board. Once happy with the cakes' position, roll a narrow sausage of white sugarpaste and place around the neck of the cat where the two cakes join. Blend the paste into the cakes with the flatter end of a Dresden tool.

2. To make the patches, roll out some of the black modelling paste between the spacers and cut one edge straight. Place the straight edge at the base of the cake and drape the remaining paste up and over the cake. Mark the shape required with a cutting wheel or knife. Remove the paste from the cake, place it on your work surface and cut along the marked line. (Removing the paste from the cake before cutting it to shape ensures a clean cut.) Stick the cut patch in place and smooth the edges with the heat of a finger. Repeat for the other patches.

Cup Cakes

Cover each cup cake with a disc of red sugarpaste. Thinly roll out some black modelling paste and place the paw-print template on top. Cut out pads with a cutting wheel and toes with an oval cutter. Arrange and then stick the paw prints to the cakes.

3. For the tail, soften some of the remaining black modelling paste by adding a little white fat and cooled boiled water. Place the softened paste into the sugar shaper with the large round disc and squeeze out a length directly on to the board (**D**). Cut to size and position as required.

4. To make the feet, thickly roll out the remaining black modelling paste and cut out a 4 x 12cm (1½ x 4¾in) rectangle. Curve the corners and glue in position. Take a Dresden tool and mark a line in the centre of the paste where the two feet join.

5. For the ears, thickly roll out some black and white paste and then roll over the paste again gradually exerting more pressure so that the thickness of the paste is reduced at one end. Place the ear template on one of the pastes with the base of the ear on the thickest area and the tip on the thinnest, and cut out the ear (**E**). Turn the template over and cut the second ear from the other colour. Sugar-glue the ears in place (**F**).

6. Mix a small amount of red sugarpaste with a little white to make pink for the nose. Thinly roll out the paste and cut out the nose, using the template. Sugar-glue in place.

7. Change the disc in the sugar shaper to the small round and squeeze out a length of paste. Cut the paste into two 4cm (1½in) and two 1cm (⅜in) lengths. With a thin paintbrush paint the mouth on to the cake with sugar glue. Then attach the cut lengths to the face to form the mouth.

8. For the eyes, roll a 1cm (⅜in) ball of black paste and cut it in half; this ensures that the eyes are the same size. Roll each half into a ball (**G**), then a cone and then pinch the larger end of the cone to taper it. Attach in place.

9. Insert the dried whiskers into the cake, adjusting their length as required. Randomly add a few indentations with a cocktail stick to represent more whiskers.

10. Finally, attach a black ribbon around the board to finish the cake.

Puss in Boots

Create boots for your cat and transform him into Puss in Boots. Model the toes from black sugarpaste, and then add black boot uppers. Finally, make a decorative buckle and gild with edible gold lustre dust.

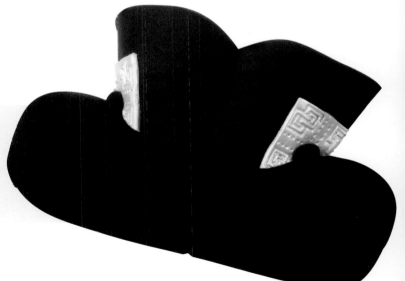

The Runaway Train

S mall children love trains, and the old steam engine holds a huge fascination for children of all ages. This brightly coloured runaway goods train carries sweets in its open-topped trucks and rumbles over sweet-decorated tracks. The variations possible for decorating the engine and trucks are endless and give plenty of scope for personalizing the cake. The cake is quite straightforward to make, but you will need to give yourself enough time to decorate the truck cakes carefully.

Materials

sugarpaste (rolled fondant): 1.1kg (2½lb) grey, 425g (15oz) black, 1.25kg (2¾lb) red

Madeira cake made with 6 eggs and baked in a 23 x 18cm (9 x 7in) rectangular cake tin (pan) (a multisized cake pan is ideal) (see page 10), **or** 4 store-bought family sized Madeira cakes, and 1 store-bought mini-roll

sugar glue

modelling paste: 100g (3½oz) purple, 100g (3½oz) black, 100g (3½oz) red, 100g (3½oz) yellow, 100g (3½oz) orange

white vegetable fat (shortening)

granulated sugar

black edible dust colour

assortment of red, yellow, orange and black sweets (candies)

1 quantity buttercream

Nonpareils Sprinkles (W)

Equipment

38cm (15in) round cake board

circles to be used as templates, such as a cake board or tray: 33cm (13in), 20cm (8in)

craft knife/scriber or dressmakers' pin

greaseproof paper

long straightedge (at least 38cm (15in))

fine paintbrush

sugar shaper with small rope and half-moon discs

spacers: narrow spacers made from 1.5mm (¹⁄₁₆in) thick card, 4mm (⅛in) spacers

multi-ribbon cutter tool (optional)

cutters: zigzag cutter (FMM), triangle cutters, piping tubes for small circle cutters

cocktail stick (toothpick)

waxed paper

circle cutters: 5cm (2in), 2cm (¾in), 1cm (⅜in)

orange ribbon and non-toxic glue stick

PREPARATION

Covering the board

Roll out the grey sugarpaste into a large circle and use to cover the cake board. Trim the paste flush with the edge and place to one side to dry.

Preparing the cake for freezing

Remove the crusts from the cake (if using home-made cake) and level the top of the cake (home-made and store bought) to a height of 6.5cm (2½in). Freeze overnight.

STAGE 1

Marking the board

1. Mark the track placement lines by placing the 33cm (13in) circle centrally on the dried cake board and scoring around it with a craft knife/scriber or pin and then repeat with the 20cm (8in) circle.

2. To find the centre of the board. Place the board on some greaseproof paper and draw around it to make a paper template. Cut out the template, fold it in half and half again. Unfold and place on the board. The centre of the board is where the two folds cross; mark this with a craft knife/scriber or pin.

3. To mark the position of the sleepers, take the long straightedge and place it across the board so it goes through the centre point. Scribe two sleeper lines where the straightedge crosses between the track lines. Repeat, positioning the straightedge at right angles to the first position and then at 45 degrees. Then add a further two lines between each of the scribed lines to give a total of 24 **(A)**.

A

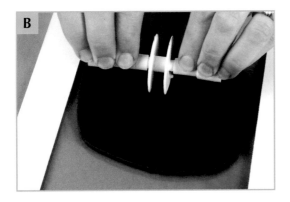

Decorating the board

1. Place sugar glue over the scribed outside track using a fine paintbrush. Soften some purple modelling paste by adding some white vegetable fat and boiled water until the paste has the consistency of chewing gum. Place the softened paste into the sugar shaper with the small rope disc, and squeeze out a length. Place over the glued track.

2. For the sleepers, roll out the black modelling paste between the narrow spacers then cut the paste into 1cm (⅜in) wide strips. A multi-ribbon cutter is useful, as it saves a lot of time and ensures that each strip is the same size **(B)**. Place glue over the scribed sleeper lines in the centre of the track, and position the strips, cutting them to the required length.

3. Add the second track using the sugar shaper as before, then add 1cm (⅜in) squares of black modelling paste to the outside of the tracks to complete the sleepers.

4. To make the gravel, place some granulated sugar in a plastic bag and add some black edible dust colour. Shake the bag to colour the sugar. Add more dust or sugar if necessary to adjust the colour. Cover the area in and around the tracks with sugar glue and sprinkle over the sugar using a teaspoon **(C)**. With a dry brush remove the sugar from the top of the sleepers and track.

5. Paint sugar glue over the centre of the board and around the edge, and then arrange a selection of sweets in a pattern **(D)**.

Tip

You could personalize the cake by using sweets of the same colour to write a number or initial in the centre of the board, and then filling in the background circle with contrasting colours.

Carving the cake

Using the carving guide, cut the frozen cake(s) into rectangles as indicated. All the cakes have a width of 6.5cm (2½in), the three trucks have a length of 9cm (3½in), the coal truck 6.5cm (2½in), the engine base 11.5cm (4½in) and the driver's cab 2.5cm (1in). Cut away the base of each truck on each side to a depth of 1cm (⅜in) and height of 2cm (¾in) and do the same for the engine. Curve the top of the cab and reduce the height of the engine base to 4cm (1½in) **(E)**.

Tip

You may find it helps to make templates of the different sections of the train and arrange these on top of the cake(s) before carving.

Covering the cakes

1. Place all the cakes, except the cab cake and mini-roll, upside-down. Spread a thin layer of buttercream over the cut-away base area of each. Roll out the black sugarpaste and cut into 2.5cm (1in) wide strips. Wrap a black sugarpaste strip around the base of one of the trucks so that it covers the entire underside (**F**). Cut the paste flush with the base and sides of the cake. Repeat for the other trucks and the engine. (Don't worry too much about the finish, as most of this paste will be hidden.)

Tip

Put the frozen cakes in the refrigerator until each one is needed.

2. Roll out some red sugarpaste and place it, reverse side up, on waxed paper. Cover the top of one truck with buttercream and place on to the sugarpaste. Cut around the cake (**G**), then remove both the cake and cut paste from the waxed paper. Cover the tops of the remaining trucks and engine in the same manner.

3. To cover the sides, roll out a strip of red sugarpaste and place it, reverse side up, on waxed paper. Cut the strip to a width of 6cm (2⅜in). Cover the sides of one truck with buttercream, then place the truck on the sugarpaste so the black base is aligned with one edge of the strip. Roll the cake up in the sugarpaste. The join should be on one of the narrow ends and the paste should stand proud of the top of the cake to create a well to hold the sweets. Smooth and adjust the paste as necessary. Repeat for the remaining trucks. For the engine base use a 2.5cm (1in) strip. Leave to dry.

Cup Cakes

Cover each cup cake with a disc of red sugarpaste. Attach orange and black modelling-paste circles and top with a yellow sweet. Paint a line of sugar glue around the edge of each circle, and then pick up and place Nonpareil Sprinkles (W) around the circles using a fine brush.

4. To cover the cab, roll out some black sugarpaste and place it reverse side up on waxed paper. Cover the front of the cab with buttercream and place on to the sugarpaste. Cut around the cake then remove both the cake and sugarpaste. Cover the back of the cab in the same manner using red sugarpaste. Spread buttercream over the remaining uncovered area of the cab then cover with a 3.5cm (1⅜in) strip of red sugarpaste.

5. Cut the mini-roll to a length of 6.5cm (2½in). Cover the mini-roll with a thin layer of buttercream. Roll out a strip of red sugarpaste and place it, reverse side up, on waxed paper. Cut the strip to a width of 6.5cm (2½in). Place the mini-roll on the sugarpaste and roll it up then cut away the excess. Cut a 5cm (2in) circle from the red sugarpaste and attach to one end of the mini-roll. Place the cake on its uncovered end on waxed paper and leave to dry.

STAGE 2

Decorating the trucks

1. Roll out the black, yellow and orange modelling pastes between narrow spacers and cover with plastic until ready to use to prevent the paste drying out. Using the suggested cutters and a cocktail stick, design and create your own patterns on each of the carriages **(H)**. The trucks can be as elaborate or as simple as you like, and can be easily personalized with a birthday message using letter cutters.

Tip

Remember that piping tubes make excellent small circle cutters.

2. Soften some red modelling paste by adding white vegetable fat and boiled water and place in a sugar shaper together with the half-moon disc. Squeeze out a length of paste and attach to the top of one truck. Repeat for the other trucks.

Decorating the engine

Roll out some red modelling paste between narrow spacers and use to cover the black sugar paste of the cab, trimming the paste flush with the sides. Take a 2cm (¾in) circle cutter and remove two windows to reveal the black paste beneath. Attach the cab to one end of the engine and the boiler (mini-roll) in front. Model a flattened round ball of yellow modelling paste and attach to the front of the boiler to give it the characteristic dome shape. Decorate the train with modelling paste and orange-and-red Nonpareils Sprinkles. Then add a funnel, dome and bumpers (I).

Finishing off

1. Place the cakes in position on the board. Roll out some orange modelling paste between 4mm (⅛in) spacers and cut out 2cm (¾in) wide circles for wheels. Add 1cm (⅜in) red circles to the centre of each and cut away a small section so they fit under the carriages (J), and then stick in place. Join the carriages together with strips of black paste to represent the couplings.

2. Add your selection of sweets to each carriage; use either one colour per carriage as I have done or mix and match. Attach a ribbon to the board.

Short Cuts
- 🚆 Make fewer trucks.
- 🚆 Reduce the amount of decoration on the trucks.
- 🚆 Simplify the board.

Flower Train
The colour scheme and decoration of this cake can easily be varied and adapted. For little girls who love trains and all things pink you could try this pink and yellow combination.

Templates

*T*o use the templates, trace over them on to greaseproof paper or white paper and then transfer the template to the sugarpaste or cake as described in the individual projects. Use the templates at the size shown unless instructed otherwise. Cutting and carving diagrams are included to help you cut cakes into sections and carve intricate shapes from frozen cakes.

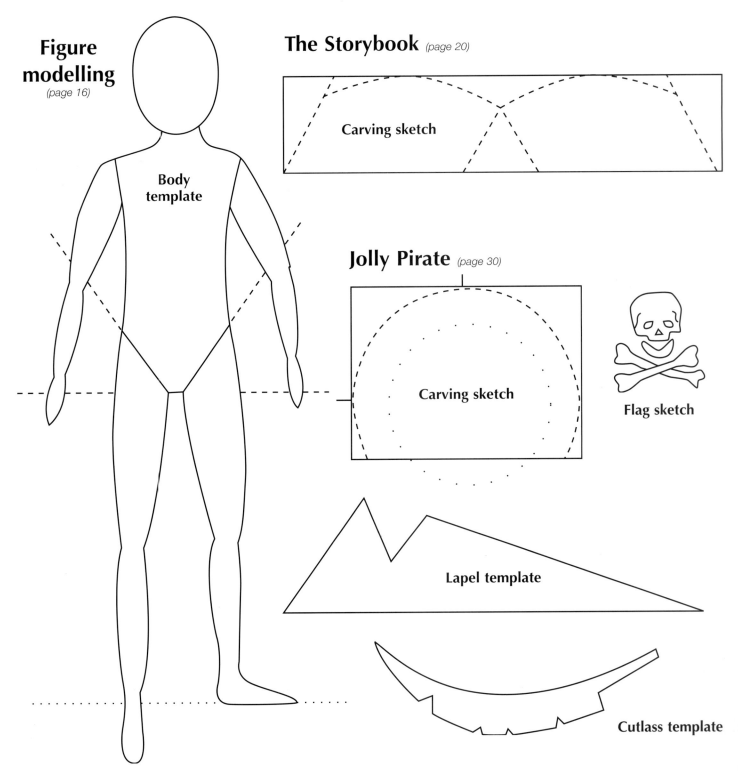

Figure modelling *(page 16)*

Body template

The Storybook *(page 20)*

Carving sketch

Jolly Pirate *(page 30)*

Carving sketch

Flag sketch

Lapel template

Cutlass template

The Frog Prince *(page 26)*

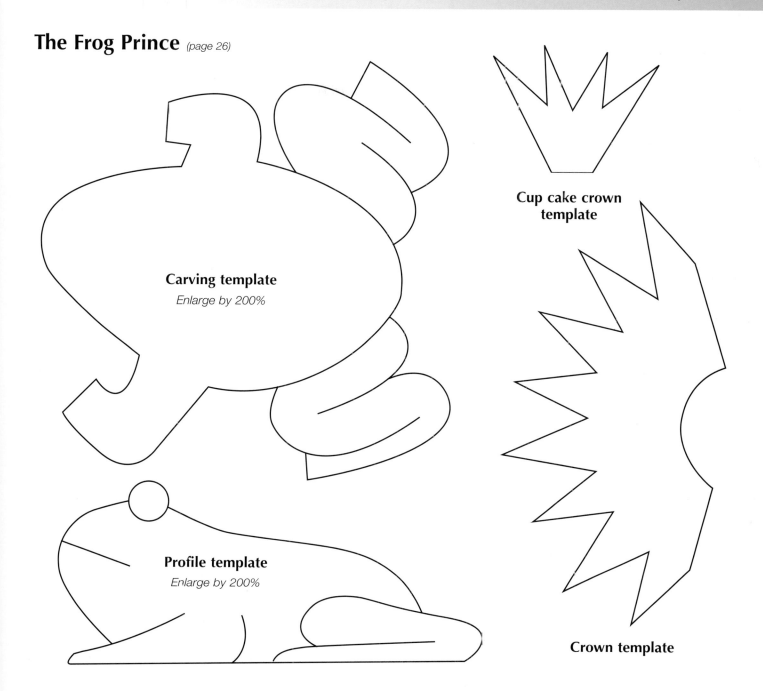

Carving template
Enlarge by 200%

Profile template
Enlarge by 200%

Cup cake crown template

Crown template

King Arthur's Castle *(page 36)*

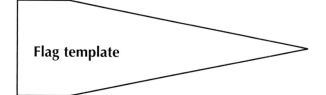

Flag template

Little Mermaid *(page 46)*

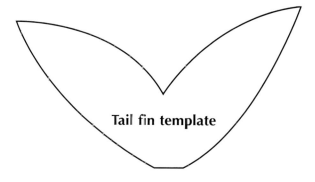

Tail fin template

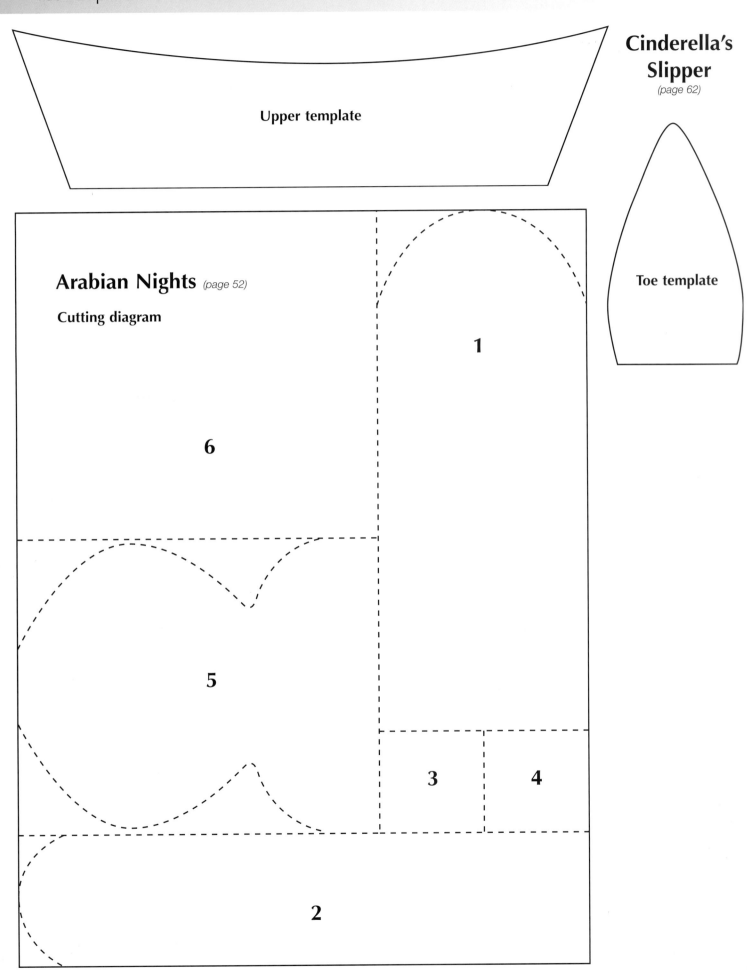

Upper template

Cinderella's Slipper
(page 62)

Toe template

Arabian Nights *(page 52)*

Cutting diagram

1

6

5

3   4

2

Cinderella's Slipper
(page 62)

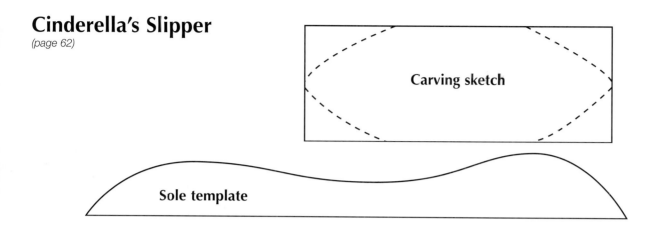

Carving sketch

Sole template

Ballet Slipper
(page 67)

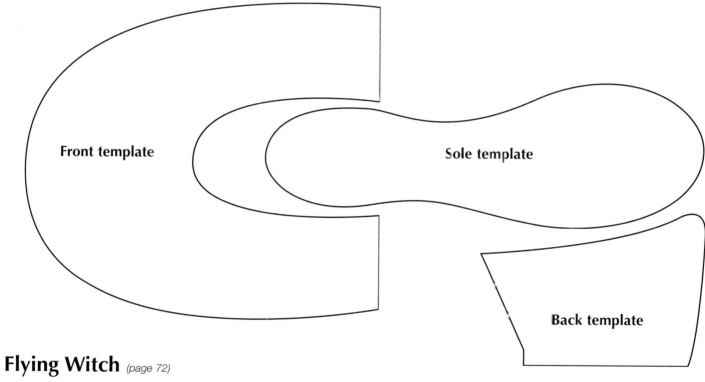

Front template

Sole template

Back template

Flying Witch *(page 72)*

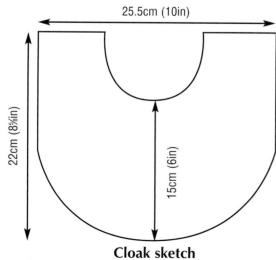

25.5cm (10in)

22cm (8⅝in)

15cm (6in)

Cloak sketch

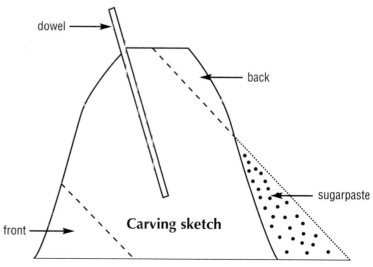

dowel

back

sugarpaste

front

Carving sketch

Teddy Tales
(page 68)

Carving template
Enlarge by 200%

Ear template

Woodland Fairy
(page 82)

Wings

The Runaway Train *(page 92)*

truck	truck	truck	
Carving guide			
engine	cab	coal truck	

Unicorn Myths
(page 78)

Cake placement sketch

Carving and scribing template
Enlarge by 200%

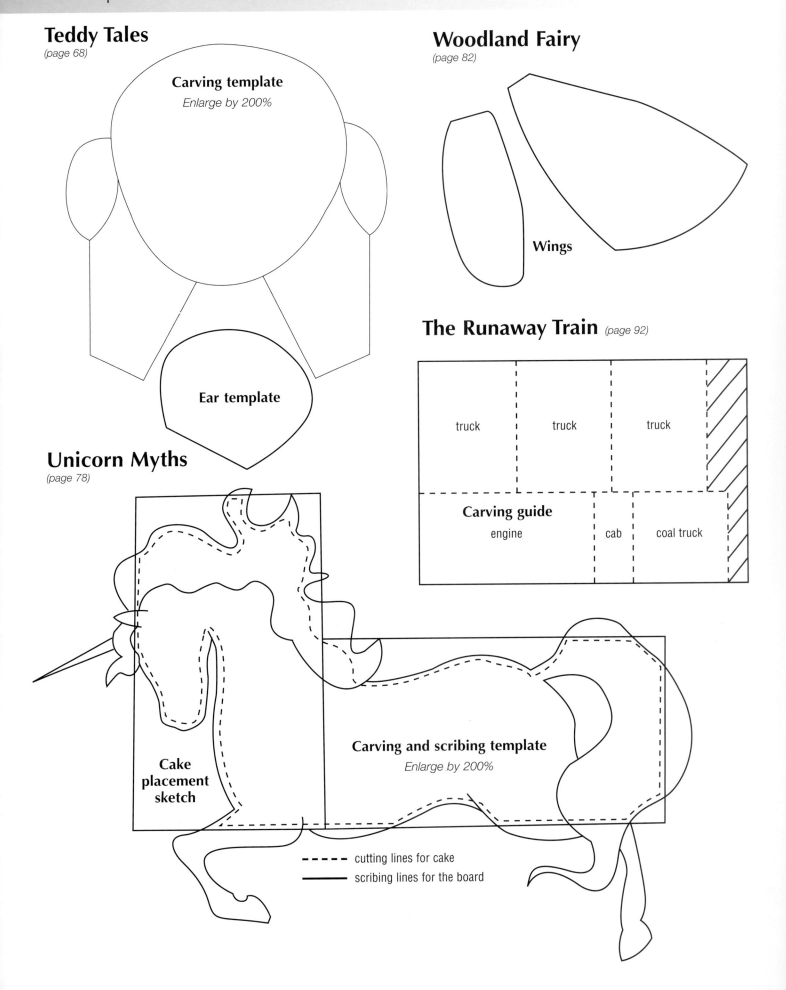

- - - - - cutting lines for cake
——— scribing lines for the board

Dick Whittington's Cat (page 88)

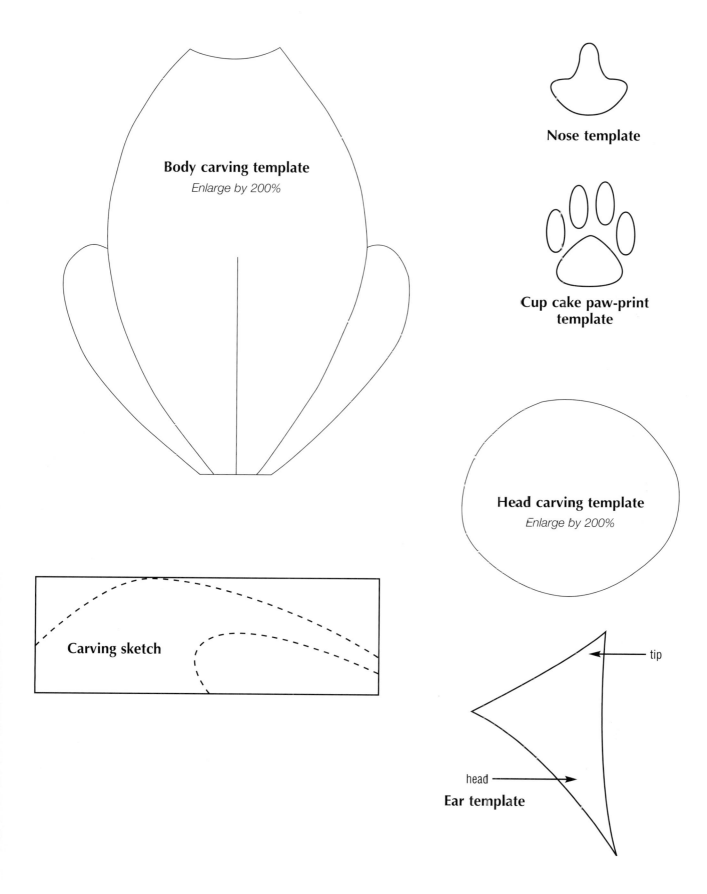

Body carving template
Enlarge by 200%

Nose template

Cup cake paw-print template

Carving sketch

Head carving template
Enlarge by 200%

tip

head

Ear template

Acknowledgments

I would like to thank M&B Specialised Confectioners Ltd for supplying me with their superb range of coloured sugarpaste. As always, it has been great to use and has saved me hours of colouring time. I would also like to thank Patchwork Cutters for being so generous with their wonderful cutters, FMM Sugarcraft and Diamond Paste & Mould Co. for supplying me with their useful cutters and moulds, and Wilton Industries, Inc. for giving me the opportunity to experiment with their sprinkles and providing the book-shaped cake pan for photography.

A special thank you goes to my family, especially my children Charlotte and Tristan, for their help, comments and suggestions. I would also like to thank Sofi for lending me her ballet shoe to copy and Ceinwen, my helpful neighbour, for ferrying the children back from school on photoshoot days and helping out with childcare when I was needed elsewhere.

Suppliers

Abbreviations used in the book:

FMM   FMM Sugarcraft
HP   Holly Products
SS   Simply Sweet
W   Wilton Industries, Inc.
PC   Patchwork Cutters
DP   Diamond Paste & Mould Co.

UK

Alan Silverwood Ltd
Ledsam House
Ledsam Street
Birmingham B16 8DN
tel: +44(0)121 454 3571
email: sales@alan-silverwood.co.uk
manufacturer of multisized cake pans, spherical moulds/ball tins and tiffin tins

Ceefor Cakes
15 Nelson Road
Leighton Buzzard
Bedfordshire LU7 8EE
tel: +44(0)1525 375237
email: ceefor.cakes@virgin.net
www.ceeforcakes.co.uk
supplier of strong cake boxes – most sizes available

Diamond Paste & Mould Co (DP)
78b Battle Road
St Leonards-on-Sea
East Sussex TN37 7AG
tel: +44(0)1424 201505
email: dpmco@btinternet.com
mould manufacturer/supplier

FMM Sugarcraft (FMM)
Unit 5, Kings Park Industrial Estate
Primrose Hill, Kings Langley
Hertfordshire WD4 8ST
tel: +44 (0)1923 268699
email: clements@f-m-m.demon.co.uk
manufacturer of cutters

Holly Products (HP)
Holly Cottage
Hassal Green
Sandbach
Cheshire CW11 4YA
tel: +44(0)1270 761403
email: june.twelves@u.genie.co.uk
www.hollyproducts.co.uk
supplier of head moulds and textured rolling pins

Knightsbridge Bakeware Centre
Chadwell Heath Lane
Romford
Essex RN6 4NP
tel: +44(0)20 8590 5959
email: info@cakedecoration.co.uk
www.cakedecoration.co.uk
UK distributor of Wilton products (W)

Lindy's Cakes Ltd
17 Grenville Avenue
Wendover
Bucks HP22 6AG
tel: +44(0)1296 623906
email: mailorder@lindyscakes.co.uk
www.lindyscakes.co.uk
mail-order supplier of much of the equipment used in this book

M&B Specialised Confectioners Ltd
3a Millmead Estate
Mill Mead Road
London N17 9ND
tel: +44(0)20 8801 7948
email: info@mbsc.co.uk
www.mbsc.co.uk
manufacturer and supplier of sugarpaste

Patchwork Cutters (PC)
3 Raines Close
Greasby
Wirral
Merseyside CH49 2QB
tel: +44(0)151 6785053
supplier of cutters and embossers

A Piece of Cake
18–20 Upper High Street
Thame
Oxfordshire OX9 3EX
tel: +44(0)1844 213 428
email: sales@sugaricing.com
www.sugaricing.com
store and mail-order decorating supplies

US

Beryl's Cake Decorating and Pastry Supplies
PO Box 1584
North Springfield
VA22151 0584
United States
tel: +1 800 488 2749
website: www.beryls.com

Country Kitchen
4621 Speedway Drive
Fort Wayne
Indiana 46825
United States
Tel: +1 800 497 3927 *or* 219 482 4835
www.countrykitchensa.com

Wilton Industries, Inc. (W)
2240 West 75th Street
Woodridge
1L 60517
United States
tel: +1 800 794 5866 (retail customer orders)
www.wilton.com

ABOUT THE AUTHOR

Lindy Smith is a highly experienced cake designer and author of three other cake-decorating books. This is her second book for David & Charles, her first being *Creative Celebration Cakes*.

Lindy started making novelty cakes when her children were small and still loves the challenge of creating their unusual requests out of cake. She runs a successful cake design company called Inspirational Cakes, which produces unusual and creative wedding cakes and special anniversary and birthday cakes. She has also appeared on television in programmes such as *The Generation Game* and, most recently, presented a sugarcraft series on *Good Food Live*. Lindy is an accredited demonstrator of the British Sugarcraft Guild and thoroughly enjoys sharing her knowledge with fellow sugarcrafters both in the UK and abroad. For more details please visit Lindy's website: **www.lindyscakes.co.uk**

Index